CASTING FORWARD

CASTING FORWARD
Fishing Tales from the Texas Hill Country

STEVE RAMIREZ

Illustrations by Bob White

Foreword by Ted Williams

Essex, Connecticut

An imprint of Globe Pequot, the trade division of
The Rowman & Littlefield Publishing Group, Inc.
4501 Forbes Blvd., Ste. 200
Lanham, MD 20706
www.rowman.com

Distributed by NATIONAL BOOK NETWORK

British Library Cataloguing in Publication Information available

Library of Congress Cataloging-in-Publication Data

Names: Ramirez, Steve, 1961- author.
Title: Casting forward : fishing tales from the Texas Hill Country / Steve Ramirez.
Description: Lanham : Lyons Press, 2020.
Identifiers: LCCN 2020941398 (print) | ISBN 9781493051458 (cloth) | ISBN 9781493066711
    (paper) | ISBN 9781493051465 (electronic)
Summary: In Casting Forward, naturalist, educator, and writer Steve Ramirez takes the reader on
    a year-long journey fly-fishing all of the major rivers of the Texas Hill Country.
LC record available at https://lccn.loc.gov/2020941398

♾™ The paper used in this publication meets the minimum requirements of American National
Standard for Information Sciences—Permanence of Paper for Printed Library Materials, ANSI/
NISO Z39.48-1992.

To Alice, one of the dearest souls on Earth, my first best friend, who climbed mountains with me in Italy, trekked many miles through thornbush beside me in Africa, saved me from dying of fever one night on the Masai Mara plains as a lion roared outside our tent, and stood beside me through each moment of darkness and light.

———

To Megan, my amazing daughter and fly-fishing adventure buddy, who saved my life on Peru's Salkantay trail, who watched the sunrise with me from Machu Picchu, who stood beside me as we both cast our lines into uncertainty, and who has traveled with me along each Hill Country river.

———

To the Texas Hill Country and each meandering stream and every winding canyon, who saved my life when I thought I could not keep breathing, and who spoke to me softly with birdsongs and breezes, and reminded me that "the proper function of man is to live, not to exist."

The proper function of man is to live, not to exist. I shall not waste my days in trying to prolong them. I shall use my time.

~Jack London

Contents

Foreword

IF YOU ARE AN ANGLER OR EVEN IF YOU JUST LOVE WILD THINGS AND
wild places, don't miss this important book by Steve Ramirez—poet, phi-
losopher, outdoor wordsmith, hunter, fisherman, naturalist, and United
States Marine.

It's a book with plenty of fishing for beautiful native species North
American anglers don't often encounter and, in many cases, don't even
know about. And all scenes are described in words that put you in the
streams, feeling the cool push of spring water against your waders, scent-
ing fresh earth, wildflowers, new and old leaves, hearing the songs and
calls of birds, watching hatching insects and rising fish, reacting to gentle
takes and savage strikes.

But it's not a fishing book.

It's an eloquent ode to Ramirez's beloved Texas Hill Country, a jour-
nal of personal healing, and a lesson for all anglers that there's far more
to fishing than fish—that when we pay attention to the life and geology
around fish, fishing becomes far more than a sport.

Bowling is a sport. Fishing, the right kind, is participation in nature.
"I looked toward the shoreline and watched as some white-tailed deer
watched me," he writes. "A flycatcher spied on me from a mesquite tree
branch. I watched him watching me. These are the moments I refer to as
the space in between. They are moments where nature accepts you as part
of the landscape, no longer an interloper, you have been admitted into the
club. As a fly fisherman, I am not simply an observer, I am a participant
just like the osprey and the fish themselves. I am involved in the give-
and-take, life-and-death, and new-life circles of nature."

In many ways, Ramirez is the reincarnation of my late friend John
Voelker, author of *Anatomy of a Fisherman* and the lesser work, *Anatomy*

of a Murder. Both men were fleeing lives that had wounded them, and both found salvation in wildness through angling.

Had Voelker lived in the Texas Hill Country instead of Michigan's Upper Peninsula, his famed "Testament of a Fisherman" would have captured Ramirez's central message as follows: "I fish because I love to. Because I love the environs where [Guadalupe bass and yellowbelly sunfish] are found, which are invariably beautiful, and hate the environs where crowds of people are found, which are invariably ugly. Because of all the television commercials, cocktail parties, and assorted social posturing I thus escape. Because in a world where most men seem to spend their lives doing what they hate, my fishing is at once an endless source of delight and an act of small rebellion."

And about Texas Hill Country, Voelker might have written, "[Guadalupe bass and yellowbelly sunfish] will not, indeed cannot, live except where beauty dwells."

Ramirez teaches us, as Voelker and Henry David Thoreau taught us, to revel in the beauty not just of fish but of everything around and overhead.

"Many men go fishing all of their lives without knowing that it is not fish they are after," wrote Thoreau.

"In this time, my life has grown within my newfound poverty, and I am the happier for it," writes Ramirez. "We must remember to notice the pennies. How many people drive over this lovely water, I wondered, and never notice how it shimmers in the sunlight?"

Sometimes his prose approaches the beauty of what he's describing. Example: "If you follow Can Creek far enough into the canyon you come to the limestone womb of the river, a pool of spring water bubbles from the ground, its bottom a mixture of stone and maple leaves, frogs jump, and ribbon snakes slither, white-tailed deer stand silent, and the sound of canyon wren-song fills the morning air."

And: "On this day, I walked the familiar trail along the Sabinal toward the ponds. It was early springtime, and Texas mountain laurel was in full bloom, their purple lupine flowers tumbling from beneath evergreen leaves. As I walked, I listened, for the sound of deer stepping in the crumbled leaves, and the song of warblers, and the soft hush of the river.

From time to time, I stopped and gazed into deep pools in between the shallow spots. A few green sunfish drifted, suspended in the molten glass over the pebble bottom, and on occasion, I'd spot a large Guadalupe bass holding in the faster water where the river tumbles from the ground."

Fish are furless, featherless, cold, slimy, silent, and, for most people, unseen. For the majority of Americans, including, alas, large elements of the management establishment, angling community, and environ mental community, fish don't count as wildlife. The function of fish is generally perceived as bending rods and posing skinless and scaleless on dinner plates.

I wish there were more outdoor writers like Ramirez. He understands that fish are part of a delicate and complicated mechanism extending from water to earth to air, that Guadalupe bass, for instance, are as important to Texas as, say, bison to Wyoming.

He deplores the mindset responsible for genetic pollution of native fish—such as those Guadalupe bass, some of which are being converted to mongrels by alien smallmouth bass flung like confetti around the Hill Country by professional and amateur bucket biologists.

Ramirez releases virtually all his fish, though he's not averse to killing and eating fish. He advocates animal rights but not the "animal rights" we keep hearing about on television and social media. He believes that animals, including fish, have rights to: habitat uncompromised by humans, genetic integrity, enlightened management, and humane treatment (which does not exclude killing quarry quickly and cleanly and then consuming it).

He puts it this way: "I know that many people who do not hunt or fish and who identify themselves as 'animal lovers' will never understand how someone can kill that which they love. Often, these same people, upon closer inspection, are the ones talking loudly and looking at their feet as they walk a park trail, or even more likely, they never actually get outdoors in wild nature. Their idea of nature is what they see on cable television. They call themselves animal lovers because they 'own' a dog or cat. . . . I wish these well-meaning 'animal lovers' and 'preservationists' could come down out of the clouds and join the ranks of us ethical hunters and fishers. We are participants, not observers in nature. We take responsibility for the food we eat. It does not matter if the living thing is a carrot or a cow, something gives its life so that something else can live . . . it is the way of nature."

Each stream in the Texas Hill Country has its unique beauty and personality. And for Ramirez, each is a metaphor for elements of human life and more: "Nature," he writes, "isn't just a metaphor for our true selves, it is a reflection. We should not look away. Wild rivers are the key to the landscape. They, like the atmosphere, give life. They carve canyons and carry our future into the circles that sustain us. Yet we treat our rivers and streams like slaves, to be used and forgotten. We treat our atmosphere in the same manner. If you think about it, they are one and the same."

And: "The boy I once was is far wiser than the man I've allowed myself to become. It's time to go backward until I find the original me, back at the headwaters of being alive."

Even the creatures Ramirez shares the Hill Country with are metaphors or similes morphing to metaphors: "Civilization is like a rattler; you should never get too close. It has a way of making you spill out all over the place until there's nothing left. Society tells each of us, it's for your own good . . . but that is a lie, and we each must know when to walk away."

In short, this is a book about how wild nature, encountered through fishing, heals damaged souls, how it brings out the best in people, and why its protection and recovery are essential for the protection and recovery of human nature.

A century hence, *Casting Forward: Fishing Tales from the Texas Hill Country* will be referenced in the best of North American outdoor literature.

TED WILLIAMS

Prologue

When the storm threatens, a man is afraid for his house. But when the house is destroyed, there is something to do. About a storm he can do nothing, but he can rebuild a house.
~ ALAN PATON, *CRY, THE BELOVED COUNTRY*

THIS IS A STORY OF RESILIENCE. IT IS A MEMOIR OF THE SPACE AND TIME journey of a post-middle-aged man traveling through fear and sorrow, disillusionment and enlightenment, courage and joy. It is the story of a Marine who felt relief the day he was diagnosed with PTSD, because, at least then, the nightmares had a name. Fly-fishing these Texas Hill Country rivers saved my life; I am hoping to return the favor. This is the story of the parallel journey of a twentysomething-year-old girl, my daughter, who finds herself, like her father, wondering, "What comes next?"

Reinvention is always new territory. We must determine which harbor speaks to us before we can ever hope to find "the right wind." This is the journey of two generations both fly-fishing through uncertainty. Our narrative holds value only in how it, like a Hill Country stream, may reflect your own. In reflection, we find solace and clarity, and sometimes in that moment, we feel less alone.

This is a story of a historical landscape. It is a memoir of a living, breathing place where the footprints of dinosaurs, conquistadors, Comanches, and I have mingled just beneath the clear waters. They have drifted away just as I will. What remains is this singular landscape, unknown to many, unloved by some, loved to death by others. This is a cry for my beloved country, the Texas Hill Country. It has survived eons with and without human hands. If we do not act now as a state, as a nation, and as a people, it will soon survive only in memory and through these few humble words. This is a story of love.

First Cast

Sometimes the slightest things change the directions of our lives, the merest breath of a circumstance, a random moment that connects like a meteorite striking the Earth. Lives have swiveled and changed direction on the strength of a chance remark.

~ Bryce Courtenay

When I lost my job, I went fishing.

I went fishing in part because I knew that the rivers and the hills could heal me, because I knew that bass and warblers have wisdom, and because I had no idea what else I could do. After years of putting my passion and my spirit into "my work," I had lost not only a job but also faith: in my government, in the myth of hard work and good outcomes, and, perhaps, in the voice of any god. This was, in fact, the third time in my life that I had done everything right only to have changing budgets and changing "leadership" lay it all to waste and leave me standing alone, wondering what was next and searching for meaning.

I remember the first time as I stood among the winter trees of a mid-Atlantic town with the snow falling heavily upon me, not knowing where to go. Soon after, I stood in the Yellow Breeches Creek, ice filled my guides, rainbow trout rose to my fly, and peace drifted past my hip boots. I remember the second time sitting on a rock near Cibolo Creek, feeling empty, and then I stood in Joshua Creek as the winter fog lifted with my spirits, and as I released another rainbow trout into the cold water, I thanked him for giving me back my perspective. Each time, I got right back up and worked to regain a position just like the one I had lost . . . and then came budget cuts and reorganization and the long drive home.

This time was different. This time, something broke inside me, and it flowed out into the Texas Hill Country that I love, and I knew that I had changed, but also, I knew that this was a good thing. Sometimes the universe is screaming at you. With every great challenge I have faced, and with every massive hit I have taken, I have found that, for me, nothing heals and gives perspective like spending many hours casting my line into a Texas Hill Country stream.

Even long ago, when there was that long stretch of time after I left the Marine Corps and years later, some of the things that I carried came back to haunt me, only fishing these hills seemed to save me. And now, after that last long drive home, I knew where I was going. It was then and there as I drove across the Devil's Backbone around Canyon Lake and across the hills toward the setting sun that I decided that I would fish every river in these hills and climb through each canyon before I chose my next life direction. I decided that my plan was to have no plan; I would let life come to me while just living, in the moment, without expectation. The ancients say that every long journey begins with a first step; my journey began with a first cast.

My first cast was in February at the bottom of Lost Maples Canyon. The Sabinal River is born here. It grows from springs that trickle from beneath the limestone bottoms of Hale Hollow Creek Canyon to the east and Can Creek Canyon to the west. The eastern tributary undercuts the limestone in two places: first along Hale Hollow, where stalactites can be seen in the half cave wall above the creek and ferns grow thick under the constant dripping of spring water, and second at the place where Lane

Creek and Hale Hollow Creek join to create the Sabinal River, and then a few miles farther south Can Creek joins the river as it begins its long journey toward the Gulf of Mexico.

In some places along this stretch of the headwaters, the river runs over shallow riffles, tumbling over stones and past the trunks of syca-more trees. In other places, deep, green, glass-clear pools surround great boulders, and each pool contains a scattering of yellow-bellied sunfish and the occasional Guadalupe bass. If you follow Can Creek far enough into the canyon you come to the limestone womb of the river, a pool of spring water bubbles from the ground, its bottom a mixture of stone and maple leaves, where frogs jump, ribbon snakes slither, white-tailed deer stand silent, and the sound of canyon wren song fills the morning air. It is my church. Just below the source of the Sabinal, at the place where the steep sides of the canyon open and allow the sun to reach the earth, the creek widens into a series of ponds and then eventually tumbles forty feet over the limestone cliff face and continues on toward the main branch of the river. It is to these pools that I traveled, my first steps, my first cast.

Fly-fishing in the Texas Hill Country never begins at the river's edge; it begins with the drive between and over these limestone and granite hills and, in this case, with a hike through a tree-lined canyon to the place where the river runs through it. Sometimes the drive can be a brief thirty minutes from my house to the nearest section of the Guadalupe River. Other times, I may drive for over two hours—never leaving the "island" that is the Texas Hill Country, perhaps crossing several rivers on my way to the one I am seeking.

The Sabinal is seventy-two miles from my house. My drive toward the canyon takes me through the one-stoplight town of Pipe Creek, through Bandera and Medina where I will cross the Medina River several times, and up over the very steep pass to Vanderpool, which consists of a post office and a graveyard. The entire seventy-two miles is within the confines of the Edward's Plateau. The rivers and streams are, for the most part, lined in ancient cypress trees; the headwater of the Sabinal is the one exception of which I know. The canyon that seeps life into this river is lined with sycamore trees in the round-rock places where the floodplain is open and, in the dim, deep, limestone canyons, the "Lost Maples" live, shading the water in summer, turning fire red in autumn.

Lost Maples Canyon and the Sabinal River hold special meaning for me. I have hiked this canyon and fished this river for many years. It is one of the two places where I've asked my ashes to be spread, legally or not, and the other place is overlooking Echo Canyon near the Llano River. Why not give my body to this land? Someday, I will be a maple leaf drifting.

I first came here with my Marine Corps brother Dave. We hiked along the river on the Maple Trail, and he decided that, true to his nature, it was time for a nap on top of the massive boulder where the deep pool reflects the trees. I hiked on toward the area I call Comanche Cave and then returned to find Guadalupe bass rising to mayflies and my brother rising to greet me. Dave is gone now, in the mortal sense, but I always see him smiling and waving from the massive stone. The massive stone has a crack in it, and from this crack grows a maple tree. This is resilience. This is hope. And this is a part of the magic of this canyon.

On this day, I was not here to hike; I came to fish the ponds at the bottom of Can Creek and to explore the narrow west branch of the Sabinal. This was the only plan I had since I have learned that plans are worthless; life happens as we plan. So, I strung up my rod and tied on a size 10 Olive Bead Head Woolly Bugger, put on my favorite hippers, and began the hike back along the dirt road and trail to the ponds.

The hike to where I planned to fish is about a mile from the trailhead. It is an easy walk under the maples, crossing the river a few times on the way to the ponds. It was easier to just wear the hippers rather than carry them, although the rubber-soled boots were less than silent on the trail. The *clink, clink, clink* of my hemostat and snips swinging from my chest pack beat a steady rhythm, but the birds didn't seem to mind. The air was cool, and it was too early in the year for golden-cheeked warblers, but I watched the empty maple branches and looked deep into the cedar trees just in case. I suspected that the cold winter air and water of February might keep the bass from biting, but it didn't matter; my life changed in winter, and in winter, I would begin fishing through my changing life.

When I reached the ponds, I was alone with the water. Solitude is what I was seeking, and it is exactly what I found. The river is clear, but the ponds can be dark in the deep parts. A limestone cliff forms the southernmost edge, and a grove of oaks and maples ring the northern shoreline. Backcasting is tricky anywhere along these ponds, and in some places, roll casts or sidearm roll casts are the best ways to get the fly to the fish and not to the treetops. I choose to begin at the point where the largest of the ponds begins to spill over the rocks to form the Sabinal.

I was literally straddling the river, here, only three to four feet wide. I cast into the deep, dark water, wondering if anything would be biting on the clear, cold morning. I stripped the fly once and saw the flash of a silver belly. My rod bent over double and throbbed with the weight of a fish, I didn't know what. I applied some side pressure, and it began to run, and then rise, and in a moment, a foot-long rainbow trout jumped once then twice before I landed him . . . amazed. Until that moment, I had no idea that Texas Parks and Wildlife had planted trout in the ponds. I held him briefly, his coral pink and silver glistening in my hand as I slipped him back into the water. Yes, I knew that he could not live here once the river began to warm, but for now, like me, he should live—truly.

After checking the condition of my fly, I cast once more, this time along the edge of the cliff face where I could see a submerged cedar tree. Stripping slowly at first, I picked up the line and cast once more, this time slightly out and into deeper water. A flash of coral and silver telegraphed the strike, and soon, I was tied onto another rainbow as it jumped and ran and ultimately came to my net. He had swallowed the fly deeply, and it took me a moment to reach down and unhook him . . . before I revived him along the pond's edge, and he swam free once more.

The wind had begun to pick up, blowing into my face and making my backcast through treetops more perilous. In short order, I caught my first cedar tree of the day, and it would not be my last. As I slowly began unwrapping my leader from the tree branch, I began to think of wind knots and tree-branch tangles and of how much I have learned from them. Let me explain . . . by inclination, I am not a patient man, but I have learned to give myself time. As I quickly review the things in my life that I am patient with, I can only come up with two. I am patient with those whom I love: family and friends—and most of all, I am patient as a parent. This is undoubtedly due to the feelings of love and being connected to other souls. I am patient when I am fly-fishing. Again, this has to do with feelings of love and being connected. I am at home in nature.

Wind knots, those tiny tangles that form in my leader when I apply too much force in my forward cast, and "tree-knots" that form when I do not pay attention in my backcast, teach me to be patient. I think the thing that makes fly-fishing so special is the casting more than the catching. If fly-fishing were all about catching, I would be better off to use bait or dynamite. Instead, I tie on a tiny imitation of a mayfly or a grasshopper, and I cast it into the air in tight, poetic loops until it comes to rest among the currents of the river, and like me . . . it drifts.

Sometimes, my casts are beautiful, graceful, like a dance that mixes air and water. Other times, I think about it too much and put too much effort into the cast. When I do this, my casts bounce back and tangle into wind knots or around the pole tip or even in a nearby tree. It is not beautiful or poetic. In any other instance, something like this would bring out my lesser nature: you know, the one that drives down the road in heavy traffic impatient with the pace of it all. I don't like that guy. When I'm on the river, wind knots and tree knots do not bother me. I remain in the moment, and I marvel at the intricacies of the tangled line around the willow tree branch. I calmly unwind it as I listen to the sounds of the river and the birds.

If only I could always be as I am when I encounter a wind knot or wrap my leader around a blade of grass. Perhaps if I relaxed and came to understand that life just happens and we must take the time to learn from it and unwind it all with a sense of calm acceptance. Perhaps if I make myself take notice that no matter what obstructs my forward movement, it also invites me to pause, breathe, and just be—with the sights, sounds, and sensations of the moment; in this way, each moment is like a lover's embrace: rare, beautiful, fleeting. So, I unwrap and open the tangle and free the tree to wave once more in the canyon breeze.

I have noticed that the only way to unwind a knot or a life is by "going big." If I try to force things by pulling on the leader, it tightens into something that can only be repaired by cutting the line and starting all over again. To free myself, I must open the loops, looking at it as if I were flying away from it, above it, where things look clearer and more hopeful. Once I take the time to open the loops, I can see the way forward, and slowly, patiently, I regain my line and cast once more in another direction. That is exactly what I did and what I am doing.

The wind picked up just a little into my face. I began to think of the bright days on the sand flats of the Bahamas, Grand Cayman, and Provo Islands casting into the wind trying to reach a silver streak with a tiny white fly. I side cast into the wind under the branches toward the deepest part of the pool. A flash of silver once . . . twice and yet again doubles my rod-tip and sends a rainbow into the air. Once, as the semi-tough trout ran deep into the weed bed, the line stopped as if I had caught the bottom. Something told me that life was still attached to the end of my line. I decided to keep applying side pressure, to remain steadfast and give it time. After a moment that seemed eternal, the trout came free of the bottom, and after a single aerial display of defiance, it came to my hand and then soon after slid back home. As always, I thanked him as I watched him swim away.

Perhaps if I knew that trout would be present in the ponds, I would have brought a cooler and brought them to the table. As a rule, I am a strict catch-and-release fisherman who uses barbless hooks and treats fish with a wet, gentle hand. In this case I knew that these trout would not live past early spring. Still, I'm glad I let them go. In the end, I had caught five trout before the action died. I moved on.

The sun came out and began to warm the day. I worked my way along Can Creek casting into a pool that once contained two very big largemouth bass, but they seemed to have gone elsewhere as bass sometimes do. Instead, I caught a tiny yellow-bellied sunfish and quickly released him into the pool beneath the falls. I began walking back along the path through the maple forest that my family and I call the "Pooh Bear Woods," across the stepping-stones above the pool where two nice Guadalupe bass sometimes nest in the spring, and onward toward the crossing of the east and west canyon trails.

As I came to the crossing of the east and west trails, I stopped and listened as the river, now about twenty feet wide, tumbled over rocks and under the tangle of maple, sycamore, and oak trees. For years, I've crossed the river at this point and said to myself that "someday" I'd explore what was around that bend and under those trees. I imagined secret pools with bass the size of manatees just waiting for someone willing to thread their bodies and fly-rods between the overhanging branches. There were two choices I had made as a result of my current life change. First, that my plan was to have no plan, and second, that I will no longer say, "someday I'm going to . . ."

Tucking my rod beneath my arm, I stepped into the river and began weaving under the tree branches. I scanned the river's edge for fossils and arrowheads as I looked forward for fishy looking pools. In time, I realized that the deep pools I imagined were not there. Instead, I found shallow riffles and narrow bends that held a few tiny sunfish and the unfolding of mystery. When I stepped out from beneath the canopy, I was not disappointed by reality. The important thing was, I stepped forward and experienced what was around the bend. The important thing was . . . I did not wait for "someday."

I must admit that after a lifetime of experiencing the worst of humanity I have come to love trout and river-born bass much more that I do people. There is not an ounce of deceit, cruelty, greed, or hatred in a trout . . . but then again, there is also no nobility, kindness, unconditional love, selfless courage, or honor.

I learn a great deal from fast, clear rivers and the fish that live within their molten-glass landscapes. Sometimes, I see a reflection of the vessel that carries me on this journey. I wonder who it is looking back at me with a graying beard and wind-worn face. I see the remains of sadness and laughter in that man's eyes. I turn away. I cast once more. More often, I see beyond that mere reflection. I see Truth.

I believe it is a gift that my daughter and I have in many ways embarked on the same sojourn; she at twenty-three, and me at fifty-three, both looking to strip away the detritus of outside expectations and find our own true path. Recently, she shared her feelings of concern about finding her path and after graduating from college, answering the question, "What next?" I told her that we are fishing, not catching. I asked, "What do you do when you cast your line to a likely space behind a rock or near the roots of a cypress tree along the river's edge and no strike is forthcoming? Do you quit? No, you may cast to that spot again, or you may cast to another, working the river naturally, without thought, moment by moment, until you find the place where what you seek finds you. This is what we must do, you and me." She smiled.

This is not a journey of loss but rather of gain, of being released into the streams that I have loved, whenever I could find the time away from obligations. And now, I know that my only obligation is to live truly and fully and that the rest is nothing more than bending grass upon the hills. These rivers and streams have given me so much; they have healed me so often, and now I want to give something back. I want to take the time not only to cast my line upon every Hill Country river and walk every canyon but also to know them more intimately. I want to live in that space in between the illusion we call living and life truly lived. And, I want to find the words to share with other kindred spirits of what makes these spring-fed streams and limestone and granite canyons so magical.

I seek to write of what Robert Finch called an "historical landscape," the story of a landscape that is "neither natural nor human, but an amalgam of overlapping and intermingling layers of natural process and human alterations." We are connected to our landscape . . . our home-waters; its journey is our journey. These Texas hills and the spring-fed streams within them need to be saved before we "love" them to death. This is their story. This is my story. This is our story.

As I walked down the trail listening to the birds singing in the trees, I heard the calling of a red-tailed hawk above me. Looking through the branches, I saw him circling in the warming air currents, searching for his destiny. As I watched him, I asked myself, *Do I have the courage of the hawk? Do I have the courage to live or die upon my own fortunes or failures, not wasting precious life-moments with worry, allowing life to come to me as a mayfly comes to a rising trout?* I felt privileged in that moment . . . connected . . . and I heard the reply inside me: *Yes.*

CHAPTER TWO

Joshua Creek

There is a candle in your heart, ready to be kindled.
There is a void in your soul, ready to be filled.
You feel it, don't you?

~ RUMI

THE MORNING WAS COOL, DAMP, AND NOT YET FULLY AWAKE AS I stepped up to the river. A slight fog held just above the water. The grass bent soft and wet beneath my footsteps, and the gray-skinned, ancient cypress trees stood there watching, waiting for something to happen. I stood there, too, my fly rod in hand, watching, waiting for something to happen—and it did.

I don't know why it is that some of my best days on the river have begun with waking alone in the darkness, truly alone, with that deep, empty feeling—that hollow aloneness that you cannot shake free of. It had been some time since my service in the Marines, but years later, the ghosts came to call, and I found myself afraid to sleep, knowing they would come back. A doctor helped me to chase away the ghosts, but the feeling of emptiness remained. I guess sometimes surviving is your punishment. So, you stand in the river, facing upstream with the water rushing down upon you as if it could somehow fill the hollow emptiness—and somehow, it always does. So it was one morning. I stood there, without even casting and with no trout rising, and as the water rushed past me, I knew it was washing my burdens behind me, swirling them downstream like the autumn leaves.

There is a great deal about living that trout can teach us. They teach us how to keep swimming even in a steady current. Trout know that if they stop swimming, they cease to be trout and begin to become debris, floating without purpose wherever the current may take them. Trout know that if they keep swimming, facing into the current, perhaps in the eddy of a rock, all that they need to truly live will eventually come to them. I learn a great deal from trout.

The river sparkled. Shafts of morning sunlight came through the tree limbs, fog returned home, and it was then that I saw the first rings appear upon the water; like inverted raindrops, the trout rose. A hitchhiker rests upon my hand, tiny mayflies looking for love. Aren't we all? How perfect they are, each one born of the river and then bursting into the air. Living, loving, and dying, only to return to the river—going home, just like me.

My line slid back and forth through the air. I looked back over my shoulder and saw the loop hanging, too perfect to be my fault, and then it straightened, and I sent it forward toward the rainbow I saw waiting behind the rock. He rose to the naturals, sipping them from the surface. My imitation, which was made of bits of feather, fur, and thread, drifted toward him. He turned, considered, and rejected it. I cast again.

For me, fly-fishing for trout is more about the fishing than the catching. If I was worried about catching trout, I would use bait or spinners or dynamite. But bait seems like cheating, and spinners seem like hardware, and dynamite makes a mess of the river and scares away the birds. So, I tie flies that cause me to be close to the river and thereby learn how the trout live and what they like to eat. Fly-fishing makes you live through the trout's eyes. Like the trout, you live in the water and learn of the currents. You reach up into the air to grasp that which sustains you. Fly-fishing connects you to the trout's world, and in doing so, your own.

Trout are not native to my beloved Texas Hill Country, but like the Apache, the Comanche, the conquistadors, and me, we have all called it home. Here in the Texas hills, Texas Parks and Wildlife stock rainbow trout into the Frio, South Llano, Blanco, and Guadalupe Rivers each year during the colder months of December and January. In the Texas summer, the water gets too hot for most trout to live and propagate, although it's rumored that a sustainable population lives in the cold waters below the Canyon Lake Dam. But the truth is the trout think its home, and so do I.

Not all my best trout fishing days have been in the Texas hills, and that's okay too. There was a time when I was visiting my mother when she lived along the edge of the Alleghany Mountains in south-central Pennsylvania. It was Thanksgiving morning and freezing cold and dark outside as I slipped out of the house while everyone slept. As I drove through the twisting snow-dusted roads and the sun began to rise, I couldn't help but smile as I turned off the pavement along the shores of the famed Yellow Breeches River. On any other day, the river would be full of fly fishermen politely jockeying for position. But it was Thanksgiving, and all the "sane" people were either at home asleep or sitting under a warm blanket watching the parade on television. I, on the other hand, found myself standing in a freezing cold river, snow falling, ice forming in the guides of my rod, and rainbow trout that seemed to like what was on the end of my line. It was a perfect day.

And, this brings me back to Texas. The home I share with the trout is a land of subtle beauty. Our rivers sometimes live just above the stone—skinny water where dinosaurs once roamed. Other times, our rivers seem to be made of stone, shyly waiting for the rain. When the rains come, our rivers demand respect. They are the kind of rivers that put cows in the trees and roll Buicks like cordwood. That is the magic of a Texas Hill Country river. Like life, it is ever-changing, always creating a new self, always connected to the past. And each winter the trout rise like shadows mixed with memories. They wait, patient and understanding that what will be will be, and that all that is true is this moment—everything else is an illusion.

And so I stand in the river casting back and forth, trying to lose that feeling of being alone. It is then that the rainbow rises and takes my offering. I raise my rod, and all at once, I am no longer alone. I am connected to his powerful runs, facing into the current. Silver line connects us, both fighting to live—two beating hearts. He comes to my net. I hold him gently, rocking him back and forth in the cold rushing water. "Gain your strength, dear warrior," I say. Am I speaking to him or to myself? With a kick of his tail, he returns to the river—and I go with him.

CHAPTER THREE

Colorado Bend

Let everything happen to you
Beauty and terror
Just keep going
No feeling is final
  ~ RAINER MARIA RILKE

FOR MANY YEARS, I HAVE READ ABOUT THE WHITE BASS RUN THAT comes to the Hill Country each spring. I have listened as tales were spun of fast action and hard-fighting fish. Once each year, between mid-February and mid-April, white bass swim up the Colorado and Llano Rivers to spawn in deep pools between the rocky riffles. In Texas, white bass are often referred to as sand bass or "sandies," and I don't know why we call them by that name, but sandies is pleasant to say. Each year, I have told myself that I would make the long drive up; this year, I decided to tell myself the truth.

My daughter Megan and I left at sunrise and watched the slanting sunlight illuminate the Texas hills and cause longhorn cattle and brown-and-white-spotted goats to glow along their edges at first, and then slowly, irrevocably, they were there, whole and in color, among the wildflower-covered fields. We drove the familiar twisting farm road from Comfort to Fredericksburg and then across Willow Springs toward the town of Llano.

Part of the charm of fly-fishing in the Texas hills is that the landscape changes with every turn. Another part of the charm is that each small county seat has its own historical and living personality. There are things that can be counted upon in each little town, things like water towers made of metal, courthouses made of stone, churches made of stone or wood, and people who are made of the kind of stuff that created this great country. And, there are some things that are unique to each little town . . . things you need to discover.

Comfort, Texas, is fitting of its name. It is a small Hill Country town where the Guadalupe River winds through, and its main street consists of historic buildings that mix the Old West with the German immigrant culture of its founders. It has a chocolatier, three winemakers, and a couple of good restaurants. There is a bend in the Guadalupe just on the edge of town that my historically bent mind's eye can see as a stopping point for explorers and Comanche hunting parties. Just northwest of that bend is one of my favorite fishing spots along the Guadalupe; it is a place that Megan and I have come to think of as our own.

Fredericksburg is as it sounds: an old German town; that is, it is a town founded by German immigrants, not a town full of old Germans, although I guess both statements are true. The Pedernales River runs through it from west to east. The river crisscrosses the town, sometimes flowing to the south of Main Street and Baron's Creek and then later to the north as it flows toward the Colorado. While Comfort is quiet, Fredericksburg is bustling. The birthplace of Admiral Chester W. Nimitz and the center of the Texas wine country, it brings hordes of tourists looking for history, German food, and good wine or for an escape from some god-awful place where skylines and ozone block out the sun.

The Llano River runs through the tiny town of Llano. It slides past the beautiful and historic courthouse, past the Confederate Memorial, past Cooper's Old Time Pit Bar-B-Que, and ultimately on toward its meeting with the Colorado River at Kingsland. The river is wide and shallow as it passes through town, and some of my favorite fishing spots are within a thirty-minute drive of the Llano River Bridge. In each case, no matter what small Hill Country town you drive into, more likely than not, "a river runs through it."

And although there are those places where the fishing is so remote that you had better pack a lunch and plenty of water, there are as many places where you can fish all morning and then break for a lunch of Texas Barbeque, Tex-Mex, or German food at a microbrewery. I think this works out well as part of my personal fitness plan because I can keep flexing my arm no matter if I'm casting or drinking an Enchanted Rock Red Ale. It's a tough life, but someone should live it, and I guess it must be me.

The Colorado Bend doesn't run through anything but wilderness, and that is part of its charm. When you go to the Colorado Bend, you pack a lunch and plenty of water and make damn sure your gas tank is full. We knew this, and so, as we continued north of Fredericksburg along old Route 16, we were well prepared for the long haul.

This is a beautiful drive. Spring is a beautiful time to travel to the Colorado. In February, the wildflowers haven't really come into full swing, but the mountain laurel is blooming in the higher elevations to the west, and everywhere there is the feeling of things waking up. We were trying to catch the start of the white bass run, which is in late February, hoping to avoid any crowds.

When we arrived, there were no crowds; there was only the canyon, the river, and the raptors overhead. We got our first glimpse of the Colorado at the spot on the map simply called "Bend." Like so many places in these hills, Bend consists of a few houses, a church cemetery, and a general store, and of course, the river runs through Bend. If you continue straight on the road as we did and do not cross the bridge over the Colorado, you will soon find yourself on a long dusty road into Colorado Bend State Park.

On the journey from Comfort to Bend, the Texas Hill Country changes. You begin where I live, on top of the Edwards Plateau where rivers like the Guadalupe, Medina, Sabinal, and Frio are shaded by ancient cypress trees. If you follow old Route 16 heading north along the Balcones Escarpment, the landscape slowly changes as you climb onto the Llano Uplift. Here the limestone turns to granite, the riverside grows drier, and the trees shade less and become mesquite, walnut, and pecan.

The Balcones Escarpment is a geologic fault line, although not a very active one; I have yet to feel an earthquake here. This is a rock hound's paradise where Texas topaz and llanite can be found in many cut-banks and river bends. Llanite is a unique, indigenous mineral that has quartz crystals that are blue hexagons. It is named after Llano County, Texas, the only place where it is found.

This land is full of such treasures; even the soil is rare and worth saving. We don't have dirt, we have soil. Dirt is something humanity discredits and discards. Soil is something we value. Here in the Texas hills, we have such a thin layer of soil that it is very precious. It makes this landscape more special that every tree and bush must fight to hold on and make a living here; just as the Apache, Comanche, and interloping Anglo-Germanic, Czech, Spanish, and Mexican settlers did . . . and just as I do.

In time, we began to see the escarpment rise more abruptly in the distance, the hills become wide and open, and the trees grow smaller. We had entered the Balcones Fault Plateau that eventually gives way to the Central Scrub Plains to the northeast and the Llano Estacado to the northwest. We wound down the long dirt road into the Colorado Bend State Park across the top of the canyon and descended quickly to the river.

When we arrived, we were alone at the riverside; solitude was what I had hoped for, and it was what I found. I had been concerned that due to the annual white bass run I would be sharing the river shoulder to shoulder with fishermen, some casting flies and others chucking ugly hunks of metal and plastic into the river.

When we stopped to check in at the ranger station, I inquired about the white bass. The lovely ranger with the sweet smile said, "They may be here, but I'm not sure yet. No one has reported them running up the river yet." I thanked her and said that perhaps we would be the first, ever the optimist. Fly fishermen are essentially optimists. Ellington White once wrote, "I have never yet caught a fish on the first cast, nor have I ever made a first cast without thinking I would catch a fish." I understood those words immediately.

At the canyon's end within the park, the river begins to widen and slow down as it makes its way to Lake Buchanan, where the white bass live most of the year. Just above, the river is narrower and shallower with many deep pools and shallow riffles and pocket water. As always, at first, we sat together and watched the river trying to get a sense of her rhythm and connecting to her.

I love that moment when I first step into the river. I love the coldness that braces my legs and the feel of the current washing away any connection to the empty, illusionary world we pretend is real. Most of all, I love that first cast . . . how the line picks up from the surface of the water and extends over my shoulder, how the loading of the rod connects me to the sky, and how my forward casts connect me to the river. It's nice to catch fish, but I love casting. And I love how the outside world drifts away with the current, how "big things" are placed in perspective and become smaller and smaller until they are gone.

Megan and I had separated by about fifty yards and began casting methodically to each likely pool, channel, and section of pocket water. She is the perfect fishing partner. We don't even have to be near each other to feel that we are sharing the experience . . . we can express so much with a smile, shrug, or thumbs-up gesture. Sometimes I like to just stop fishing and watch her cast. Tight loops sway forward and back, and even though she is often irreverent to the "rules of casting," her casting is a form of poetry.

Sometimes I like to stop fishing and watch the river. I look at the treetops and up the canyon wall. I look at the clouds drifting by and the flock of egrets that are swirling above me. I see the white-tailed deer drinking and hear the canyon wrens singing. An osprey flies overhead and looks at me as he passes by, two fellow fishermen at work. Watching and listening to the river is always a form of poetry.

We cast for several hours, moving first toward a deep pool at the end of the canyon and then back up toward the pocket water upstream. I didn't even see a fish. Megan said she saw a small yellow-bellied sunfish.

The water was cold, clear, and seemingly empty, although I knew the fish were there, Guadalupe bass if not white bass.

Normally, this would be the perfect time to catch the annual run. I had seen photos of fishermen standing in this very spot holding up stringers of white bass, and although I had no intention of killing any fish, the photos indicated the action that could be had if you were in the right place at the right time. Sure, it would have been nice to hit the run just right and have that memory of catching our first white bass on a fly to share together, but that day will come.

On this day, we had a beautiful morning of fishing on a wild, empty river surrounded by wilderness. We had our picnic lunch at the side of the river and watched as the Colorado drifted. We hiked down the mile and a half trail to Gorman Falls and watched spring water tumble some sixty feet over the limestone cliff into an emerald pool that then ran into the Colorado. And, when we left the Colorado Bend, we pledged to return, leaving no regrets behind us.

Perhaps the sound of water falling over stones draws us, as if back toward the womb of the world, rushing as our blood does through our bodies. These rivers are vessels of the earth that give life and ask nothing in return. Perhaps I feel at peace on the river because the sound of it all beats to the same rhythm as my heart . . . the treetop winds seem the same as those that fill my lungs. Whatever it is, I know this: Magic lives in these Hill Country rivers, and each time I turn from them, I dream of returning to them, and I pray that we never kill this magical place I call home.

My second journey to the Colorado River Bend was filled with sunshine that struck the fresh green leaves of each tree in such a manner that they reminded me of one of Monet's paintings of haystacks at sunrise. The roadside and the fields were dressed in blue, purple, yellow, red, and white . . . bluebonnets, verbena, primrose, fire wheel, and poppies. A huge caracara or Mexican eagle flew alongside the road. Once rare in these hills, they are becoming more common, as the temperatures seem to rise each year, the caracara expand their range northward.

This time, the weather had warmed, and the bluebonnets were in full bloom. I had shared my experience on the first trip, the lovely, lonely river and the lack of white bass with a gentleman who works at the local fly-fishing shop . . . we will call him Zeke, not because that is his name but because it should be. He has a large, bushy, Texas-sized mustache, and a native drawl that doesn't seem to fit his somewhat spasmodic, jerking, rushed behavior. He's not my favorite guy at the shop, but I knew that he guided for white bass on the Colorado and Llano, so I went to pick his brain. Zeke listened impatiently and then said, "Well, the old adage is, no bluebonnets, no white bass." Wise words indeed, Zeke.

Feeling good about my timing, I stepped into the river at the wide section that spreads out before falling into Lake Buchanan. The river bottoms vary in these hills to some extent depending upon the geologic location. In general, rivers of the Edwards Plateau, rivers like the Guadalupe, Medina, Sabinal, and Frio, have a hard limestone bottom with shallow-to-deep stone trenches cut into the limestone that runs parallel with the current. Sometimes, the deeper sections contain a pebble-like bottom on top of the limestone.

The rivers of the Llano Uplift, such as the Llano and Pedernales, are similar, perhaps clearer, and most always less shaded. Here in the Balcones Fault Plateau, the Colorado has a mix of hard limestone bottom with deep pools along the canyon side of the river and soft sand flats along the river's inside turns.

Walking into the river . . . crossing the sandy flats, the water was running clear and shallow. The drought that the Hill Country has been experiencing for several years and the brutally hot summers have both taken their toll upon the springs that feed these waters. Stepping slowly through the shallows, I noticed trails of sand clouds in the water that reminded me of what it looked like when I spooked a bonefish while stalking along a Caribbean flat; all that was missing was the turtle grass.

I wondered if the trails of floating river bottom were coming from nesting bass but soon discovered that fleeing carp were everywhere, some of them running in the four-to-five-pound range. In the distance, I could see large silvery fish leaping from the water, and then simultaneously, I saw the sleek bodies of carp doing the same. My pulse quickened as I asked myself, *Are those white bass jumping?*

I began casting, and as the river is wide in this spot, I did my best to bring up my line speed and extend my cast out farther into the deeper water where the silver fish were jumping. I had tied on a chartreuse and white Clouser with golden flash knowing that if this didn't work, I would try one with silver flash. Zeke had told me that these were his "go-to" flies for white bass on the Colorado and Llano Rivers.

As I came to the first set of small waterfalls and riffles, I began casting into the pool that runs up- and downstream along a limestone ridge that is just below the surface. It only took a few casts to make my first hookup with something that felt too light for a white bass. Zeke told me that they pulled hard and fought well in a bearing-down sort of way. Soon my suspicions were met with a lovely smallish bass leaping into the air at the end of my line. I brought him to hand. He was about ten inches long, full-bodied, and iridescent green. Thanking him, I set him free, and in short order, I caught a few more bass, each one full of fight and color.

By this time, I had been fishing for a few hours. Giving my arm a rest, I rested on a half-submerged boulder in the center of the river where it begins to narrow just upstream. Cool water rushed by me and wrens sang along the canyon wall. Three ospreys swooped and danced in the sky above me, and every so often, two of them crashed together in midair. It was an aerial display like I'd never seen before, and I wondered if ospreys' mate in mid-flight.

I looked toward the shoreline and watched as some white-tailed deer watched me. A flycatcher spied on me from a mesquite tree branch. I watched him watching me. These are the moments I refer to as the space in between. They are moments where nature accepts you as part of the landscape, no longer an interloper; you have been admitted into the club. As a fly fisherman, I am not simply an observer, I am a participant just like the osprey and the fish themselves. I am involved in the give-and-take, life-and-death, and new-life circles of nature.

Just above the small waterfall is a series of pools on the edge of a limestone island. I walked with as much stealth as I could muster toward these pools as the water is clear, and the fish have eyes too. Something moved as I came toward the pool . . . I held my position and searched the water for the source of the massive shadow. It was then that I saw them; five massive striped bass moving away from me in three feet of water. Now I knew what I had seen jumping in the wider part of the river. And no matter how hard I tried, I couldn't entice a strike from a single fish, no matter what fly I threw at them. Mystery solved.

In the end, I caught four of the most beautiful emerald green bass I have ever seen . . . beyond that, the fishing was wonderful, and the catching was slow. I had driven over two hours to get here in the hope of catching the famed white bass run. I had made this drive once before to no avail, and this time was no different. Either someone had failed to tell the bass that they should be upriver by now or the crazy weather and extreme drought had thrown off their timing.

Life is a series of choices; in fact, the only thing that we must do in life is die and make choices. Making no choice . . . is a choice, and inaction is an action. For years, I chose to say to myself, "Someday, I will go to the Colorado and fish the white bass run." That "someday" was waiting for me to make a choice and act upon it. This is true with everything from writing words upon a page to choosing to sit by a river and simply watch in silence, your eyes and spirit reaching out until you join with it, and in doing so, you come home.

As it turned out this year, I never caught a single white bass on the Colorado River. What I did is make a choice and act upon it, and in doing so, I have begun a journey that I will reenact each year until I truly "cross the river and rest beneath the shade of the trees." Eventually, I did catch my first white bass, just not on the Colorado. This, too, is how life is; it unfolds, not as we wish it, but as it must, and we need to have a plan of having no plan other than living authentically.

I have come to see that there is nothing that ends our spirit except for our own failure to keep it alive. Life happens, like a river's flow. Sometimes, the river flows softly, the sound of riffles and falls and birdsong bringing calm to the morning sunrise. Sometimes the river floods, ripping trees from their anchors and washing jeweled fish from pool to pool, it matters not, they make a new home wherever the river takes them.

Everything, even death, I suspect, is a new beginning. Whenever a painful thought or feeling drifts into my mind, I simply acknowledge its arrival and set it into the river to drift away. Every time I raise my rod-tip and then feel the loading of the line pulling back . . . back . . . into the past, and then feeling the power of my forward stroke, without thought, only feeling, until the leader and fly rest gently upon the water . . . I know, there are new possibilities. So, I will let everything just happen to me and just keep casting . . . no feeling is final.

CHAPTER FOUR

Pedernales

It may be that when we no longer know which way to go that we have come to our real journey. The mind that is not baffled is not employed. The impeded stream is the one that sings.

~ WENDELL BERRY

THE UPPER WATERS OF THE PEDERNALES ARE SLOW AND NARROW AND winding. I don't fish them often because they are sparse, and the countryside is open with the hills off in the distance, and I'm a solitude seeker who gravitates toward deep canyons. Years ago, when Megan was a young teenager, we fished the area near Lyndon B. Johnson National Historical Park Ranch and caught a few small sunfish and tiny fingerling bass where the river tumbles across the elevated road. Unlike most of the Hill Country streams that become more civilized with distance from their headwaters, the Pedernales begins to gain some steam and become wilder after it has passed through the wide, open valley between Fredericksburg and Johnson City. Still, even early on, it is a lovely meandering river that crosses 150-year-old cattle ranches and miles of vineyards; this is the heart of Texas Wine Country.

All historical landscapes are bound by traditions. It doesn't matter if the tradition is a Comanche buffalo hunt or German and Italian winemaking, these threads bind people together in a good way. The Texas Hill Country is a land where humanity's influence has woven cattle ranching, deer hunting, and winemaking together naturally. Each tradition brings people together within the landscape, building community through the ancient arts of living.

My grandmother was from "the old country." She grew up on a farm in the foothills of the mountains of central Italy about an hour's drive from Rome. She grew her own vegetables, baked her own bread, and made her own wine in the basement of her home that my father built for her, mostly by hand. I remember when I was a very small boy being down in the wine cellar watching my father hand turn the steel and wooden grape press, and the juices would flow down the steel funnel, and as they did, my grandmother would tell him not to spill a drop because it was precious like blood.

I loved the smell and feel of the old wine cellar. I loved how the barrels looked, all stacked in rows along the wall, and how dark and cool it was there on those hot summer days. It was like a cave. It felt primal, like an ancient home.

Sometimes when my parents would drop me off with my grandmother, we sat on the back porch in the early morning coolness, drinking caffe latte and eating biscotti. We talked about the old country and how rabbits can be evil if they are eating your garden, and she asked me to step on the carpenter ants that she felt sure were eating her porch. Later, as the day grew hotter, we went down into the wine cellar where she turned on her old black-and-white television and adjusted the rabbit-ear antennas so that she could watch her "soaps" in Spanish.

While we sat there, my grandmother took two glass tumblers from a shelf, and from the barrel or sometimes from a large glass jug, she poured two glasses of deep, ruby-red wine. After they were poured—almost as if it were a sacred ceremony—she handed me one glass and told me, in a conspiratorial whisper, "Here, this isa precious likea blood, and it'sa gooda for you, but you no tella your momma, cause she no understand." So, I took the glass, and I drank it, and I knew that she was right. I was five years old.

Since then, I have always known the power and the beauty of living from the vine. Wine, made as she made it, is not just wine. It is artful, full of tradition, respect, and even acts as religion. Like raising our own vegetables, it connects us to the land and the generations. Like killing a deer and roasting its loins, it teaches us to have respect for what sustains us. Wine, like she made it, brings people together to speak, listen, laugh, and remember; at that moment, we are all connected by blood.

In time . . . I grew older but not up. I found myself serving as a Marine at the embassy in Rome, not more than an hour's drive from my grandmother's hometown. In Rome, I met my wife, Alice. We traveled to tiny villages where we sometimes lived off the local pasta, bread, and wine. Once, in the hills outside Rome, we could only afford a piece of bread, a piece of cheese, and a liter of wine. That was one of the best meals of my life.

We had traveled to see the fountains. It rained like God's tears, and it didn't matter if the water was going up or down because it was all beautiful. That was living. And we had Italian friends named Franco and Carla. They sort of adopted me. On the weekends, we would travel to their countryside home. Once there, we would all gather around the fire and laugh, eat, and drink cool white wine poured by Franco . . . oh so carefully. He knew that it was precious.

Later, I would sit by a campfire on the African plains in northern Namibia. We looked up at the Southern Cross through the branches of the big tree that had been damaged by elephants. We ate the roasted meat of the game I had shot that day and drank deep, red, rich, African Pinotage. I sat there with the thick, wonderful, wood-smoke smell in my nostrils. That was the night Jan, Fred, and I—three warriors sharing thoughts and memories—talked into the wee hours of the morning. Jan and Fred were the professional hunters in camp, and they had previously fought against the current government of Namibia as special operations soldiers. Our trackers, Pete and Johannes, had previously tracked Cuban soldiers through this bush.

I remembered those times in my own counterterrorism wars as a Marine in West Africa when Cubans smuggled guns through Ghana and killers from Libya. We drank wine, laughed . . . and got quiet and distant inside ourselves when we talked of war and of loss. We had each defended our countries under the same African sky. We were brothers of the battle . . . brothers around the fire and within the blood. It was something precious, and we did not spill a drop.

As the years passed on, so did my grandmother. Her name was Dominica. In Italian, this means "Sunday." I remember how the sun filled her smile as she sipped the first of her new wine. I remember how she taught me that wine could bring people together. Still, I hear her voice and see her smile each time I walk into a barrel room of a winery and smell that oaky, deep, warm smell of long ago. And I'm sure that if there is a heaven, she is there pouring a tumbler of her deep, red, ancient elixir for the Lord. She was a tough old farm girl and will show him no quarter. I'm certain as she pours it, she will hand it over carefully and say, in her broken Italian accent, "Here . . . you no spilla drop. This isa precious . . . like blood. "

Now I am home in the Texas Hill Country I love so much. I look toward the hills and wonder how they could look so African. I look toward the vineyards and wonder how they could look so Tuscan. I look toward the smiling eyes of my fellow Texans sipping wine and listening to Texas swing music and wonder, *How life could get any better?* And then I stand in a Texas Hill Country river casting my line to the wind and water, and at that moment, I know life can't get any better.

———

I strung up my rod at the parking lot of Pedernales Falls State Park, about a mile or so from the river. I was alone but not lonely. Pulling on my hippers and my backpack, I began the winding walk down the trail through oaks and cedars, past prickly pears and blooming sotol toward the canyon's edge. The trail to the river is rugged and starkly beautiful. The grasses wave with the desires of invisible molecules that carry my scent toward the noses of watching deer. Wildflowers are sprinkled among the grasses; they wave, too, in colors of red, yellow, white, and blue.

I hear the sweet descending note of the canyon wren's song and the cry of an osprey in the canyon below.

The path from the rim to the river drops steeply with almost no switchbacks. I must be careful not to catch my rod on the many overhanging tree limbs. I switch my attention from the wildflowers to the expansive river view while making sure not to step off the trail where Newton's gravity will have its way with me. At the bottom of the canyon, the riverbanks are covered with fist-sized rounded stones and boulders the size of minivans.

I sat for a long while just watching the water slip by, looking for mayflies or any other activity on the surface or in the air. I notice the plunge pools and the deep runs, devising a simple strategy to toss a streamer across the current. I tied on a white and Chartreuse Clouser Minnow and walked into the river. The canyon was empty, except for me and the river and the osprey and all the rest of the universe.

Casting can seem like breathing. At its best, there is a natural rhythm, like lovers matching breaths; I match my casts to the swing of the river's currents. It's like playing the blues: natural, flowing, present, and without thought. It only took a few casts into the first pool to connect with a bright yellow-bellied sunfish and then a small but determined bass. He dug into the current at first and then gave a nice aerial show with a couple of dancing leaps across the water. Rainbow trout jump; Guadalupe bass "tail-walk" on the water. I brought him to hand and marveled at his deep emerald-green and black ornamentation before returning him to the current.

Working along a submerged limestone ridge, I connected to several more sunfish and another bass slightly bigger than the first. I took one more cast into that current, and my rod bent in a determined but dull manner, more like the pulling of a winch than a living thing. The sunfish fight in an aggressive, throbbing way so that you can feel their will to live. This fish simply pulled toward the deeper water. In time, I brought him up. I wasn't thrilled to find that I had caught a channel catfish, but I treated him with respect and eventually got the hook out without harming him or getting stabbed by his dorsal fin.

I've caught them before on the upper Guadalupe, and I've seen them on the Frio. Even though they have that nice slate-blue color, I don't like dealing with them. As a kid, I had one stab me deep into my thumb. At first, I didn't see it and thought I had been bitten by a cottonmouth. It bled terribly and stung like crazy. Ever since then, I'm careful with catfish.

The catfish tore up my Clouser, and even though I had no reason not to just tie on another of the same, I decided to switch to an Olive #10 Krystal Woolly. I was there for the fishing and the solitude, and as such, I was casting in that casual way you do when you have no desire for technicalities. Sometimes my favorite times are when I stop fishing and sit on a rock in the middle of the river . . . just watching. If you're not careful, you can miss out on everything. Don't get me wrong, I love being in the zone and catching fish. Still, I also know that part of it all is being out there at the bottom of the canyon in sweet solitude listening to the sound of the river and the song of the wrens.

I noticed a nice plunge pool below a riffle that ended in a small waterfall. Casting across it, I let my streamer swing, and after a couple of short strips, I found myself connected to my second favorite fish in these hills beside the Guadalupe: a Rio Grande cichlid. These jeweled fish love undercut banks and plunge pools. I don't catch them very often but have picked up a few on the Medina and Llano Rivers. They have thick lips and multicolored coats, and they feel like studded snakeskin in your hands.

Each one I have caught has fought as if it were four times the size of the actual fish. Besides the color and perhaps how rarely I catch them, I guess it is their attitude that makes me love them. I've noticed one more thing about Rio Grandes . . . I always catch them in the most beautiful spots on the river. Like me, they seem to appreciate the scenery.

The Pedernales cuts through a landscape of history. Even its name is from the Spanish word for flint stone and is attributed to the fact that Native Americans of this region were drawn to this river for the quality of its stone. The main branch and each tributary all served as quarries for the creation of arrow- and spearheads. I've read that this stone is 300 million years old, which, to my mind, sort of puts my own insignificance in focus.

The Spaniards arrived in the mid-sixteenth century, first establishing a mission among the Lipan Apache who lived here at the time and then, later, fought battles against them and the Mescalero Apache once things began to fall apart. Peoples of various tribes, including Apache, Comanche, Spanish, Mexican, Germanic, and Anglo-Saxon, all have come, and some remain. I wish we were more artistic than engineering oriented. We need to love this land for its empty spaces. It is the silence between the notes that matter.

After releasing the Rio Grande sunfish, I walked upriver, taking notice of the stones hoping to find an arrowhead. Looking up, I noticed a deep pool of slower-moving water with an undercut bank. There were huge old cypress trees along the bank and pocket pools between the raised limestone ridges that cut down the center of the river. I saw some good-sized bass smacking the surface but couldn't see what they might be eating. Because of the deep darkness of the water and the size of the bucket-mouthed boils, I assumed there were largemouth bass in this lazy stretch.

Switching back to a Clouser, I began casting to the undercut and swinging the streamer into the meager current. After about fifteen minutes of fishing this pool, I moved on, having caught absolutely nothing. The top-water action had ceased even before I could wade over to it. No matter, it was a beautiful slow stretch of river.

I worked my way up the river, slowly, methodically casting into runs and plunge pools catching a small bass or sunfish here and there. This was that kind of casual fishing I sometimes do where catching doesn't matter to me as much as being there in such a beautiful place. When I do this, I often stop and stand in the middle of the river, just seeing and hearing and being.

Seeing is not the same as looking. I see without expectation. Hearing is not the same as listening. I wait for nothing in particular. I do not fill in the silent moments. Being is not the same as existence. Being is when you let go and realize that there is no difference between you and the air, water, or even birdsong. We are all the same atoms rearranged for current convenience. The space dust falling upon me each day is my homeland. The only things that are foreign to me are those rearranged by humanity.

The first time I ever really saw the stars, I was fourteen years old. My father and I crossed over to Green Turtle Cay in the Bahamas to spend a week living for the most part off the sea. You can't do that in many places. This was a long time ago, in the mid-1970s, before Green Turtle was anything other than a conch outpost.

When we took the chugging ferry across to the Cay from Abaco, we pulled up to the docks feeling hungry from our journey, so we bought oven-warm Bahamian bread slathered in real butter. We ate it like cavemen at the docks with the sweet, salty smell of the sea in our noses and the warm comfort of black Bahamian coffee boiled in a battered tin pot with eggshells floating mid-current. It tasted like adventure.

That week we dove for fish, conch, and lobster each day, and by the time the week was over, I couldn't stand the sight of it. We had lobster in our morning eggs and in our midday salad and then broiled with butter at dinner every day. We had lobster in fritters and salad and on crackers, and as wonderful as this was at first, by the seventh day, even God would need a rest.

At sunrise, I would sit outside watching the sky change colors from purple-black to blood-orange-red and, ultimately, turquoise. As the sun rose, I sat by the yuccas as the myriads of hummingbirds came to the tall, ivory spires. Then each evening, weary from a glorious day at sea, I would play guitar as the sun drifted over the westward horizon and the stars appeared until there was almost more light than dark. I remember looking up in amazement each night and wondering why the sky was such a secret and asking myself how I could stand living once again where the lights of humanity extinguish the lights of the universe. Those starlights remained hidden until I saw them again in Namibia, Peru, and West Texas.

The first time I ever really tasted water, I was a twenty-three-year-old Marine. I was hiking in the mountains of Abruzzo in central Italy. It was the first time I saw brown bear prints in the snow and chamois along the mountaintops. When I began the climb, I met an old man who was pulling a log out of the forest with a mule. I spoke to him in my broken Italian and asked him about the bear, wolves, and chamois. He pointed up the trail and gestured that all I was seeking could be found along that path. In a way, he was right. Then before parting ways, he told me that I would be crossing a mountain stream and that it was important that I taste the water. He cupped his hand to his mouth and said, "Dolce."

I am grateful that I met this old man and this mountain stream before I learned to fear drinking unfiltered, wild water. I reached the stream as it tumbled over moss-covered stones beneath the shade of the beech tree forest. I cupped my hand as he had done and drank from the stream . . . it was sweet indeed. In fact, I couldn't stop drinking it. I emptied my Marine canteen full of Roman tap water into the ground and filled it at the streamside. Until that moment, I never knew what water tasted like.

The first time I realized that death didn't matter, I was twenty-four years old. I was a US Marine Sergeant in Africa and had spent several years in two continents being tracked and tracking Islamic terrorists. When I was twenty-three, I wasn't going to frat parties; instead, I was carrying an Uzi and a pistol with a top-secret security clearance.

My best friend was killed in Lebanon, and others had died along the way. What was frustrating wasn't the danger, it was the government not allowing us to do our job and go after them. By the time I was twenty-three, I had looked directly into the eyes of a jihadi terrorist who wanted to kill me. That was 1984. No, this is not a new war . . . same killers, different generation. I began to learn more over time about mortality and, more importantly, about living each day as it is: a gift.

Once, I spent a night dying of some tropical fever in a tent in Kenya. A lion was roaring outside my tent all night as I drifted in and out of consciousness. While I was laying there feeling sure I would not see the sunrise over the Mara plains, I realized the great calm I felt inside. No fear, nothing but gratitude. Even at twenty-four years old, I knew that I had lived an amazing life.

In the morning, the lion wasn't roaring anymore. I drank thick, black Kenyan coffee outside my tent as zebras and impala grazed. It wasn't my time. When it is, I will cross the river; until then, I'm still on a mission. These words are a part of that mission. Life means nothing; living means everything. Understanding the space in between this world and the next humbles you. I remember flying over the Sahara of Libya looking down for an hour at endless nothingness and thinking, *I'm just a grain of sand.*

Sometimes I feel as if I could lie down in the river and dissolve back into my original elements. Only humans try to cheat nature. I have no interest in airtight boxes and let my dust scatter into the tree limbs and tumble into a spring-fed stream. Let the dragonfly young feed on my scattered particles, and over time, I will fly in streaks of sapphire-blue effervescence across the riffles once more. Nothing can ever be taken away from us; we must give it away. And, since we own nothing, this is the right thing to do.

Being thoughtful isn't helpful. It gets you nowhere, like one of those roundabouts where you can never seem to get left. The Buddha was speaking truth when he said, "It is better to travel well than to arrive. Even death is not to be feared by one who has lived wisely." When I stop thinking and start being, I feel more at peace. After all, I have thought my way into every painful quagmire I've ever had to wade through. Like when casting, if I don't think about it, the loops naturally roll off the end of my rod. The trick is to untangle mental wind knots.

"It may be that when we no longer know which way to go that we have come to our real journey. The mind that is not baffled is not employed. The impeded stream is the one that sings." These words speak to me, you see; I didn't just lose a job, or a career, or people I once cared for and trusted, or faith in divine intervention, or faith in my government, or belief that I could work my way to any goal no matter the circumstances, although I did lose all of these things. I also lost the desire for the life direction I once coveted. I lost the illusion that I control infinite time and space through sheer will. Still, what I have gained is freedom. I have gained the ability to let go and allow life to unfold as it will . . . accepting everything as it is, expecting nothing. I now know that none of us know what's next, we just think we do. And that's okay.

Walking back toward the parking lot, I could hear the roar of tribal oblivion. At the beginning of my walk, there was only the sound of warblers and winds bending golden grasses. There was only the sight of bounding white-tailed deer and budding prickly pears. There was only the feeling of my footsteps on the earth and the sky coursing through my lungs. Then, as I grew ever closer to the parking lot near the swimming hole, I could hear the loud voices of people who had no business being here.

At the lot that was empty upon my arrival, I found trucks, cars, and school buses occupying every space and every roadside edge. Down the opposite trail from the one I had taken, there were hundreds of high school kids yelling and screaming and splashing and missing the whole point of this place and the stories it contains. Yes, I know that they were having fun cooling off in the river. Still, they might as well have gone to a public swimming pool where only the city squirrels and English sparrows would have to endure the senseless noise.

Grateful that I had enjoyed a morning of solitude, I unstrung my rod and drove away. I didn't know where I was going next. It didn't matter. My former path was the wrong path, and now, with that way impeded, I could find a place to sing.

Chapter Five

Medina

*But if these years have taught me anything it is this: you can never
run away. Not ever. The only way out is in.*
~ Junot Díaz, *The Brief Wondrous Life of Oscar Wao*

The Medina is the one river that I have fished backward. I'm
not sure if it has been purposeful, but I most often explore a river by fishing it from the headwaters down until I reach the place where it either
empties into a reservoir, lake, or another river. Sometimes I fish a river
until the water no longer calls to me because it has grown thin and murky
from the unquenchable thirst of humanity.

The first time I fished the Medina, it was at Red Bluff Creek many
years ago. There used to be a dirt road that followed along the creek
until it came to a small house where an old woman lived alone at the
place where the creek meets the Medina and where the Medina spills
into the lake that holds its name. Medina Lake is a deep, man-made
reservoir that feeds water to San Antonio and the mesquite-scrub ranch
lands to the south of the Hill Country. The dam was built in 1911, and

the 1,500 Mexican hands that built it ultimately formed the town of Mico; its name is derived from the Pearson's Medina Irrigation Company that funded the dam and built the original workers' camp where the town now resides.

When I was a young man fresh out of the military, my Marine Corps brother Dave and I used to swim in Medina Lake. Back then, the water was deep and the lake was filled with stripers, white bass, and enormous catfish. Now, Dave has been gone for almost a decade and a half, and the lake is nearly dead from all the pipes that drain it and the river that feeds its impounded shores.

The first time I fished the Medina, I drove up and parked at the old woman's house in the place that was reserved for fly fishermen. She came out to my truck in small fragile steps and spoke in a kind Texan manner.

"Howdy," she said.

"Good morning, ma'am," I replied, wondering if she was a long-ago Aggie.

"Gonna do some fish'n?" she asked.

"Yes, ma'am, with your permission," I responded.

"I ask two dollars for the parking," she said softly.

"May I offer four? I appreciate your kindness."

She smiled, took the dollar bills from my hand, smoothed them out in a slow, formal manner, smiled again, and said, "Good luck," as she turned away, walking slowly back toward the screened porch of her old house at the end of the road.

The trail from the old woman's house ran along Red Bluff Creek to the river. It wound across the bluff at first, weaving through brush and grassland until it descended to the Medina. As I climbed down from the bluff, I could hear water crashing over rocks. The river here is narrow and fast, with the spring-clear stream water spilling over and around great boulders and knotted roots of cypress trees.

For reasons I cannot recall, I had come that day with only one fly box, and inside were all dry flies, including some diminutive terrestrials. The Medina is the one river in the Texas Hill Country where I have experienced long, lovely mayfly hatches. They are small, yellowish mayflies that always make me wish I was more versed in Texas river entomology, something for my "to do" list.

When I had worked my way down to the river, I jumped across, hopping from boulder to boulder, then back again after walking along a very snaky-looking patch of brush until I was standing in the middle of the crashing flow that struck the rock, splitting in two and tumbling into a deep plunge pool. I stood there feeling the mist rising from the three-foot waterfall landing on my face and the sound of cardinals singing and the smell of rain coming up from the Medina. Then, as now, at that moment, there was no world of humanity with all its grasping ways. There was only me and my five-weight rod, a Royal Wulff dry fly, and the river.

A sidearm cast to the first plunge pool brought an immediate strike; there was no need to worry about a good drift. The river is narrow here as it is for most of its course, so in short order, I had a small Guadalupe bass in hand. I love Guads as much as any fish and more than most. In fact, I may love Guadalupe bass the most of any fish I know simply because they are found here and only here.

They are the perfect canary in the coal mine species for these beautiful and unique hills and the spring-fed streams that cut through them. Yes, I love to catch trout, and just like so many other souls who cast a fly rod, I am forever captivated by the power and speed of bonefish. Still, if I could be the voice of any fish on Earth and call out to the world about their intrinsic value and somehow chain myself to a canyon to stop the advance of developers building houses for snowbirds, I'd do it for the love of these lovely fish and the place we call home. I guess that is exactly what I'm doing now.

The Guadalupe bass is endemic to the streams and rivers of the Texas Hill Country. It lives nowhere else on Earth, and this is one of the things that make it so special. Another charm is that the Guads all think that they are trout. While the big ones of two to maybe three pounds will live in deep riverine pools, the smaller Guads hold in fast water using rocks and cypress knees for cover. Like trout, they will sip mayflies and terrestrials off the surface. They fight like trout fight, using the current to their advantage and giving aerial displays, perhaps jumping three or four times before being landed. Guads will also go on cross- or downriver runs, and a two-pounder can give you a real fight on a five-weight rod.

When young, Guadalupe bass can have a lovely emerald-green color with light-dotted striping along their white bellies. The main threats to them are not osprey or kingfishers but rather the blundering ways of humanity. The rivers are in danger from dams and pumps that draw water for farms, ranches, and thirsty cities. The fish are in danger from the actions of long-ago Parks and Wildlife biologists who thought their job was providing gamefish for sportsmen rather than protecting the gamefish that were already calling these hills home. Introductions of smallmouth bass have caused a hybridization problem only now being rectified slowly. How much better could this world be if we could just learn to leave it alone?

Sometimes, even often, I will catch fingerlings on mayflies, terrestrials, or even large streamers. When I catch a five-inch Guadalupe on a three-inch woolly bugger, I always remark that they are "overachievers" and tell them to "go grow up" as I release them. There is a certain degree of perceived cockiness to young Guadalupes. They always seem somewhat incensed by the indignity of being caught. I love it when I catch fingerlings. It means that the river is still healthy and the next generation is on the way.

As I continued to cast upstream, I worked around each large rock and root trying to be stealthy as I was walking downstream toward the lake. For the most part, I caught yellow-bellied sunfish with that easy kind of relaxed fishing you do when you are there for the river and not for any worldly accounting of success. It always makes me smile when someone sees me coming off a river with rod in hand and asks me, "Did you catch any big ones?" It's a natural question, I guess, and I love catching a big fish as much as anyone, but in truth, if all I catch is time on the river . . . I'm happy.

—◆—

Over time, I followed and explored the Medina away from the lake and toward its source. The next place I came to be was English Crossing. The first time I fished English Crossing it was very early in the morning and a mayfly hatch was coming off the water, each tiny sailboat glistened in the morning sunshine even as they took to flight. The dawn air sparkled across their wings, and fish made smacking and sipping sounds as some of the duns became breakfast. There was no other sound save for the echoing call of a canyon wren, the hush of the water running over shallows, and the sipping of sunfish and Guadalupe bass.

I watched the river for a while, as I often do, and then inspected the mayflies drifting. A lovely, yellowish size fourteen landed on my hand, and I went about trying to match the hatch as best I could by holding flies from my box up next to the one on my hand. When it comes to entomology, fly selection, and presentation, I have a long way to go. Still, my shortcomings in these areas seem to matter little when fishing for forgiving sunfish on a Texas stream.

I am reminded of a favorite quote by Allison Moir: "I look into . . . my fly box and think about all the elements I should consider in choosing the perfect fly: water temperature, what stage of development the bugs are in, what the fish are eating right now. Then I remember what a guide told me: 'Ninety percent of what a trout eats is brown and fuzzy and about five-eighths of an inch long.'" With this in mind, I first selected my best imitation of the bug on my hand, but ultimately, I knew I will catch most fish with something "brown and fuzzy and about five-eighths of an inch long."

The first few casts brought nothing, but after a few good drifts, a strike brought a small Guadalupe to my hand. Over the next fifteen or twenty minutes, the hatch continued, and I continued to catch small bass and large yellow-bellied sunfish, each one bright and beautiful. I had been casting toward the cliff face, and as I rounded a bend in the river, I turned and began making sidearm casts under the cutback. At first, there was only the casting and the sound of birds. Then, a popping sound rang out, my fly disappeared, and the fight was on. I didn't know what I had hooked into, but it didn't jump like a bass, and it pulled harder than a normal yellow-bellied sunfish. I played the fish until it was within reach of my landing net, and it was then that I was surprised to find a beautiful, heavy-bodied Rio Grande cichlid in my hand.

The Rio Grande cichlid, also known as the Texas cichlid, is a species of the lower Rio Grande drainage from Northeastern Mexico into Texas up to its northernmost range in the Hill Country. It is the only cichlid species native to the United States. Rio Grandes have a grayish, high-backed body with bright-blue upraised scales and two dark spots, one at the center of the body and another at the end of its tail. Adult males have a large hump on their heads, and they feel stocky—thick and powerful when held in your hand. I rarely catch Rios, but when I do, I am thrilled. They fight hard with a plow-through-the-water determination that belies their small size, and to my eye, they are intricately beautiful.

I should mention that in Texas we call the Rios and all the smaller non-bass sunfish "perch." Yes, we know they are not biologically perch, but that's what we call them, so if you fish the Texas Hill Country . . . learn the language, ya'll. If you're not from Texas, then you should take the time to enjoy temporary immersion in our culture. What follows are some helpful tips.

Slow down and enjoy life; this is not New York City, and there is no need to hurry anywhere. Be kind, patient, and polite; life is short, and mutual kindness makes the trip more enjoyable. Enjoy our food, vineyards, and music, but please don't tell us how much better things are in California or buy a cowboy hat and wear it with running shoes. If you do, we will be forced to revoke your visa and send you home. Welcome to the Lone Star State, ya'll. It's a whole other country, and we like it that way.

Besides Guadalupe bass, these rivers contain native northern largemouth, spotted, and introduced smallmouth bass. The introduced bronzebacks have become the major threat to the existence of Guadalupe bass because they crossbreed. Texas Parks and Wildlife is now trying to fix the potential disaster they created. Human intervention in nature is seldom a good thing, no matter how well-intentioned it may be.

Farther downriver, there is a deep, deep pool. After the water spills over a small fall, it bubbles across the pool, where two monstrous northern largemouth bass live. I cut off my dry-fly and tied on a size 8 Olive Bead Head Woolly Bugger. Hidden behind a great rock, I cast as gently as I could across the pool letting my line swing with the current and then stripping it back to me in jaunty jerks, hoping to entice a strike. The big bass ignored me as if they were supermodels and I was the guy with the high-water pants.

I decided to take that one last cast, the one you always take to the pool you already fished because faith told you there had to be something down there, and besides, it was such a pretty spot. As the woolly began to swing with the current, my line went taut, and a two-pound largemouth leaped into the air shaking his head furiously. He ran across the current, using it to his advantage, and I applied pressure, trying to work him out and wear him out. Two more jumps, and it happened   I saw my line floating in the air over my head, the tippet snapped, the fly was gone, and the fish was free. Disappointed but happy, I laughed. It still counts. It was just another long-distance release.

——

Fly-fishing is my meditation. It is one of the only times that I am not a prisoner to my thoughts. Sometimes I think I was cursed with a brain. I try not to think about it, but still, I think all the time. It's like having the wrong remote control for the television. It doesn't matter if I hit stop, pause, reset, or mute . . . I keep thinking. I tried actual meditation, but all I did was sit alone in the dark, thinking about making sure I did it right. I'm thinking about trying it again someday.

Thinking isn't all it's cracked up to be. Sometimes, thinking can get in the way of doing. If we had to think about making our hearts beat or lungs breathe, none of us would last long. The things that we do best are always the things we just do naturally. I remember when I was a kid playing football. If the quarterback threw me the ball and I thought about it, I would always drop that sucker. I felt like Charlie Brown . . . a lunkhead. If I just did it, no thinking, just "in the zone," it was as if my armpit was magnetic. It was as if the ball was flying home all by itself. I always caught it.

Have you ever noticed that cows never worry about the butcher shop? They just eat grass and munch their cud, all facing in the same direction or lying in the shade of a tree. I would make a lousy cow. I would ruin the whole thing, and none of the other cows would like me. I just could not help myself. Eventually, I would walk up to the herd and say, "Hey ladies, do you know where this is all going?" I doubt any of them would even look up. Instead, they would continue to eat and sleep, and I would be alone in the back forty planning my great escape.

When you're cursed with a brain, it's hard to be thoughtless. The best things I have ever done, I did without thinking about them. For example, I joined the Marines because I felt it was the right thing to do—for me. Many people who loved me, and many who did not, thought it was a mistake. I was told that I would never do it, that it would be too tough. I served as a Marine for five years, and they were some of the best years of my life. During that time, I learned what it was to be a part of something noble. I learned the true meaning of the words "honor," "courage," "service," and "love." During that time, I learned what it meant to be a man.

Later, when "life" was taking an ugly turn and all my thoughtfulness paid off with a big goose egg, I decided to go hunting in Africa. It was a childhood dream, the kind of thing that everyone says, "Someday, I would like to . . ." Whenever I hear someone say those words, I know they will never do the thing they are considering. Instead, they will think about it, find all the reasons why they can't, or shouldn't, and then they will go back to grazing.

My African adventure made no economic sense, and it was worth every penny. I hunted and hiked from the Kalahari Desert to the Skeleton Coast. I climbed the world's tallest sand dune and slept beneath the Southern Cross. I laughed with Bushmen trackers and sang the "kudu song" with my professional hunter as we stumbled through the mopane bush at night. It is a good thing I didn't spend much time thinking about it. I did it because I felt that my life would be so much the lesser without it.

Several months had passed since the unexpected bend in my life's stream, and all in all, I was doing a good job of being thoughtless. I had, for the most part, stuck to my plan to have no plan to treat life as it is, just time on the river. My daughter has been in a similar place; after graduating from college and a stint in Peru working on an archaeological site, she was left with the question . . . "What next?"

One night when this nagging question was getting the best of her, I listened to her concerns trying very hard not to act like a guy . . . you know, an annoying problem solver. When she was done sharing, I said, "You and I can't force this . . . we must treat it like we are on the Medina working our way downstream. We don't anticipate, we don't worry, we don't think . . . we just keep casting." Sometimes, I wonder if fish ever worry. I don't think so. I think they are smarter than that.

—◦—

Summer was in full swing when next I found myself standing in the early morning sunlight at the edge of the Medina River near Ranger Creek. I had the river to myself, as most people were indoors sitting under an air-conditioning vent. With the heat and the low water, I decided to tie on a little popper that I had bought a long time ago just because it was pretty. I had never used it before this day. It was painted black and yellow like a bee, as were the tail feathers.

Ever the optimist, my first cast brought an instant strike. It was a big yellow-bellied sunfish with a bright egg-yolk color to his belly and long black "ears." I thanked him and set him free; this was a good start to my morning. I knew what I needed, so I took my own advice and just kept casting in that leisurely manner that says, "No pressure," because any day on the river is a good day, fish or no fish.

The little bumblebee popper was making up for lost time. In fact, I couldn't stop catching yellow-bellied sunfish. All the time it had spent hanging out in my fly box, unused, and now it seemed as if it knew that this was its day to shine. Within a half hour, I lost track of how many sunfish I caught: ten, fifteen, twenty, and then it went into the "what does it matter" range. I released yet another brightly colored sunfish and paused long enough to feel that the weight of the world was gone. I was casting and catching, alone within myself, feeling good about being alive. It was then that I noticed that I was not alone.

Standing on the bank watching me fish was one of the most beautiful young Asian girls I had ever seen. She was that sort of graceful lovely that some women have, like a wildflower, like a breeze in the grass. She smiled at me, and I said softly, "Good morning." She smiled again and said even more softly, "Good morning," before she turned and walked away.

I wondered how long she had been there watching me as I continued to cast and catch, as I spoke softly to each fish, thanking them and complimenting them on how beautiful or handsome they were depending on their apparent gender. I wondered what she was thinking as she stood there watching me fish in that peaceful meandering way. Come to think of it, I don't think she was thinking at all. She was just being lovely, like a mayfly.

When she vanished, I was alone again, just me and the river and the memory of a lovely crossing. I had worked my way upriver until it narrowed and changed from being wide and flat to being narrow and fast with small plunge pools at every new bend I explored. A white-tailed deer stood up in the grass next to me and then bounded off. I could tell that she had been watching me too. The breeze was singing along with the redbirds in the cypress treetops, and the sound of cicadas filled the air, calling out as they do when the days become very warm.

The trick now was to walk with stealth toward each little pool and to take the time to just watch and see who lived there. In places, the river was a mere five feet wide and tumbling fast over rock and root. Then I would follow it up until it widened to perhaps three or four times that width, still calf-deep shallow in most places but with pools that went between four to eight feet deep. At the outlet of one of these pools, I watched as a small school of five-inch fingerling channel cats swam in circles for no apparent reason other than the sheer joy of it. And then I came to the magic pool.

The magic pool received its name in my mind's eye as soon as my own eyes looked upon it. At its center was the ancient stump of a long-gone cypress tree. I wondered if it was cut down by some pioneering settler who honed and shaped its heart into the beams of a cabin roof or a chair to sit upon. It must have been cut, I thought, when the river's course was slightly to the left or right. In this time, the pool of water around it was deep and clear with small falls rolling into and out of it. At the knobby base of the old dead tree was a bass, green and spotted with black diamonds, as beautiful a bass as I've ever seen.

Planning my cast, I drew back, sending the line just beneath the canopy that formed a tunnel of green over the river. Swinging forward, I dropped the little bumblebee popper just upriver of my target and let it drift over toward his hiding place. When it arrived, I saw him look, or more exactly, I could feel him looking. I gave it a twitch, and it popped slightly and then vanished into the vortex that was his gaping mouth. He fought valiantly, giving me a few runs, but with nowhere for him to go after a jump or two, he was in my wetted hand. I thanked him, and I set him free. He was beautiful, and I was completely at peace, connected, and yes, even joyful. It was a perfect day on the Medina.

Being a Marine, I never run away from anything, not ever. Sometimes, I might back up, regroup, and advance in another direction . . . that is what they taught us on Parris Island: never give up, adjust, adapt, improvise, and overcome. This doesn't mean that I or anyone should ever keep doing the same thing repeatedly expecting a different outcome. It means that we must learn along the way, forgive ourselves if we fall, and make new choices.

Sometimes, the way forward is not clear. Sometimes, life's path seems like a river after a heavy rain: turbulent and turbid. This is as it should be. It's not about the catching; it's about the fishing. We must keep casting forward to each likely place, taking what comes our way and always searching deep into our own reflection for our own "truth." We must remind ourselves that sometimes, the only way out . . . is in.

CHAPTER SIX

Sabinal

Eventually, all things merge into one, and a river runs through it.
The river was cut by the world's great flood and runs over rocks from
the basement of time. On some of those rocks are timeless raindrops.
Under the rocks are the words, and some of the words are theirs. I am
haunted by waters.

~*NORMAN MACLEAN*

THE CANYON THAT IS FORMED BY THE HEADWATERS OF THE SABINAL
River is a magical place for me. It is where I went when my soul felt
disconnected with the death of my best friend, the loss of another best
friend, the loss of my life's direction, the loss of faith, the vanishing of
illusion. There are brightly colored fish suspended in the water at the
bottom of the canyon; their ancestors watched as Comanche and Apache
warriors drank from cupped hands. They sipped mayflies from the surface
as generations of lost maples dropped crimson-colored leaves to float, in
tandem, like a hundred silver and golden sailboats in the breeze.

Most days, the water seems narrow and gentle as it tumbles over limestone toward the sea. It doesn't seem possible that a stream that you can step over at the narrow places could also become the river that cut this deep canyon over time. There is a mountain lion that drinks from the river at the spot where the canyon opens, and the river widens into a series of ponds. He has been seen by the rangers lying in the brush, waiting for thirsty deer. We share this river and this canyon, him and me. We do not mind.

Canyons are places where time bends and twists, rising and falling, spilling and unfolding like the streams of water that carve them. They are the space in between the illusion we live in and the reality of all that lives beyond our mere senses. Canyons are spirit places. If you listen, you will hear the echoes of those you once loved and of the person you once were, and it is then that you realize that you will always love them . . . they will always be with you, and you will always hold within you the spirit of that far away time. Canyons are magical like that.

I have walked through canyons across many miles of the Texas Hill Country. For me, if there is an entity that so many humans call "God," then that God lives in these canyons. I could never find universal eternity within the walls of a building or the shallow veneer of a congregation of equally lost souls. If I want to see something that speaks of eternity . . . I must go deeper. I must walk across the limestone that over time erodes and drifts away like so many youthful dreams and under the cedar trees that cling desperately, patiently, knowingly, to the canyon wall. I understand them, and they know me all too well.

In this canyon that was formed by the Sabinal River, bigtooth maples are said to be lost. They, of course, have never been lost . . . they are home. The only lost souls in that canyon are the tourists that drive in to see the leaves and fail to see the trees, the river, and the echoes of past lives . . . the canyon. The canyon at Lost Maples is a special place for me.

When I returned from dangerous times, serving as a Marine—back when I was a younger man with still older eyes—I came to this canyon with my best friend from the Corps, Dave. We served together and lived through it all by fortune or grace depending on the theology we chose. As we walked along the canyon floor, we talked of the past, enjoyed the moment, and looked down the winding trail. We didn't know then where the trail would take us or how long we had left to walk across its weathered stone, facing into the wind.

Later, we climbed to the rim of the canyon and sat on a boulder overlooking the river. Dave told me what his wishes were when the day came that he might cross the river and rest under the shade of the trees. Dave died that year. He was only forty-one, but like me, he was so much older. Now when I return to that canyon and sit on the rock, Dave sits with me. Canyons are magical like that, too.

Anyone can write about mountains. Everyone seems to want to look at them from afar and then climb them so that they can then look back to where they stood in the first place. Mountains are lovely, but canyons teach us more. So many people only think of canyons as something to look into or climb out of. Like the mountains, they stand at the canyon's rim looking down and away. They cannot see that our lives are more enclosed, more immediate . . . here and now, not there and another time. Our lives are carved by the streams of experience. We meander along the path of least resistance and tumble toward our tailwaters.

The Texas Hill Country is a land of rivers and streams and, therefore, a canyon land as well. I have walked Echo Canyon between the two great granite domes of Enchanted Rock. There, the wind that constantly blows across the rock is silent, and the trees seem to be waiting for something to happen. As I pause to look within, I wonder how many souls have stood where I stand, be they Comanche or cowboy, settler or sojourner. I wonder if they noticed that it is not only the rock that is enchanted.

Often, I stand in the rivers that form the canyons. As I cast my line back and forth and allow my mind to drift with the fly, I pause. The descending song of a wren calls from the canyon wall. I listen to it reminding me that all the cares of humanity are insignificant, illusions that we all agree to believe in. I look up, not down, and see the many layers of history carved into the rock. Standing in skinny water, the same water that carved the canyon, I smile. Life is good. Time is bigger than me. I will come, and I will go, but the canyon will remain. The river will flow without me, and someday, someone else will stand there listening to the descending song of my friend's progeny.

So, when the time comes that I am to cross the river and rest beneath the shade of the trees, I will return to the canyon lands of the Texas Hills. And someday, another soul will climb a rock that overlooks the river, looking at the falling autumn leaves and the blooming white flowers . . . and I will sit with them. Canyon spirits are magical like that.

On this day, I walked the familiar trail along the Sabinal toward the ponds. It was early springtime, and Texas mountain laurel was in full bloom, their purple lupine flowers tumbling from beneath evergreen leaves. As I walked, I listened, for the sound of deer stepping in the crumbled leaves, the song of warblers, and the soft hush of the river. From time to time, I stopped and gazed into deep pools in between the shallow spots. A few green sunfish drifted, suspended in the molten glass over the pebble bottom, and on occasion, I'd spot a large Guadalupe bass holding in the faster water where the river tumbles from the ground.

There is a place just after the ponds where the canyon bends with the river and the river goes underground. Sycamore trees line the white-rock rubble of the dry riverbed, their roots still swimming in its current. And then, the earth drops about twenty feet in elevation, and the river pours out of the stone and forms a deep, clear plunge pool just below the falls. There was a large bass living in the pool, and for a long time, I tried to catch him, almost hoping that I wouldn't. I never did.

Whenever I am here at the birthplace of the Sabinal, I always try to live in the moment. And when I am casting and sometimes catching what I cast toward, I do, in fact, live from one deep breath to another. But this place is inhabited by ghosts, and I see them when perhaps no one else can; they are, after all, my ghosts.

I always see Dave sitting on the massive streamside bolder, waving at me with a big smile on his face. I see a much younger image of my daughter as she caught her first fish here, how she smiled brightly, and how we embraced in our happiness when he swam away. And, when I hike up to the top of the east canyon rim and sit on the edge of the cliff overlooking the river, I see myself long ago sitting in that very spot on my vision quest. I remember opening my eyes, immediately cognizant that I was being watched. Standing, I saw a massive horned mouflon ram watching me. We considered each other for a moment, and then he seemingly stepped off the cliff into oblivion, and I never saw him again. Still, like a rare few people, he will always be a part of my life. His ghost lives within me, and I see him in my mind's eye each time I sit upon the canyon's edge.

Often, I feel more connected to wildlife than humanity. With people, the greatest connections I have ever known required no spoken words, and this is also true with fish and birds and deer and even small green lizards. The Sabinal is one of those rivers where you can mix fishing with hiking. I love this as I get to feed both passions and find myself encountering so many lives that remain forever emblazoned in my memory. There was the juvenile Texas rat snake I found crossing the path to the river and the sleek ribbon snake that was hunting in the first gin-clear pool and there are banded water snakes that swim head-up across the ponds. Even when they are not there, I see them as I pass the spot where they once were.

I have noticed a change in the lizards that live here. Twenty years ago, all I would see was the spiny lizards along the lower trail and among the cedar trees and Texas mountain laurel at the top of the canyon. In the deep river canyon among the maples, I'd see green anoles, and once along a rocky trail there was a massive alligator lizard that watched me carefully as I passed by on my descent toward Can Creek. But things have changed with the rising of temperatures and the drying of the river. Now everywhere I notice the arrival of earless lizards that before I had only found in the driest parts of the Llano river floodplain. It's not that I mind them, it is only I wonder what it means.

There was a time when I had to cross the headwaters at a wide spot among the sycamores by stepping from one big, half-submerged rock to another. I would have to be careful because the water rushing by tumbled with the force of exuberant nature across this space, and I did not want to get carried away with my own natural exuberance. Now, this same spot is a vast dry white-rock path where earless lizards that were once never here dart to and fro with their bright-banded, up-curled tails. The waterfalls that I once sat beside are now only memories. The pools where I caught Guadalupe and largemouth bass are simple depressions in the stone. Sometimes these ghosts haunt me. Will they ever reappear? I think not.

In the Hill Country, the trees speak to me as well. Trees can remind you where you are and what it means. One of the many things that make these Texas hills special is that they are the easternmost or westernmost limit to that range of several species of trees. Here along the banks of the Sabinal is the only place in the Hill Country where bigtooth maples line the river. If, over time, this canyon continues to become hotter and dryer, these "lost maples" may truly be lost. Here, too, in the places where the canyon opens wide, the westernmost population of American sycamore grow with their mottled bark flaking off in great irregular parchment sheets, drifting onto the river below, massive spreading limbs shade the water, cool the canyon, and fibrous roots grasp for the thin rocky soil as the canopies they support reach toward the hot Texas sun.

Elsewhere across the Edwards Plateau bald cypresses grow, shading miles of riparian landscape, shading fish-filled rivers such as the Guadalupe, Medina, and Frio. In winter, their leaves fall, scattering like millions of mayfly wings into the water, adding to the mix that feeds the river that feeds the aquatic insects that feed the fish. I have read that some of these ancient cypress trees are as much as 1,000 years old. I wonder as I cast my line beneath them how many generations of fish and fishermen have these trees shaded. I'm grateful that most have been spared the sawblade.

Across the rivers of the Llano Uplift, pecan trees grow along the San Saba and the Llano where deer and turkey gather when autumn brings manna from above as pecans drop to the earth. Then, there is the San Marcos, where it spills out of the hills and into the central plains, its banks covered by an impenetrable green wall of box elder trees that I have seen nowhere else. Wherever I go in the Hill Country, the trees remind me where I am.

Even the stones speak to me here. The cliff face is of jagged limestone, and the riverbanks are covered in its rounded white offspring. Arrowheads, hand axes, and fossil seashells tell their stories, and in some places where the river runs dry, the footprints of dinosaurs remain exposed to the same sun that once warmed their creators. Multicolored pebbles cover part of the river bottom, and in other places, wavy ridges of slippery-smooth limestone speak to the generations of water drops that have come this way. If the stone is the canyon we can see and grasp, then it is the river that is the canyon we feel.

The Sabinal is a river I always fish without any sense of urgency. It calls me to rest, to cast wherever I choose, and to let the fly drift as it may. I fish everything here: streamers, poppers, terrestrials, dry flies, and, sometimes, rarely I will float a nymph over a waterfall and into a plunge pool. The ponds at the headwaters are a challenge except in the winter when the Texas Parks and Wildlife Department fills them with stocker rainbow trout that are fun to catch on streamers but ultimately doomed. By April, the water is too warm for them to survive. If at the end of the season you take them home and eat them, they taste like stockers: man-made. Still, I have grown to love them, and they fight as if they will live forever in their new homewaters. I guess we have that in common.

In the ponds live some massive examples of the native largemouth bass. It is difficult to cast in most areas and even more difficult to catch as these fish have grown big by not being caught. I have also found them to be choosy at times, only feeding on one insect that is at that moment prevalent, a behavior not uncommon with Guadalupe bass but that I have not observed elsewhere with largemouths.

The best way to fish these ponds would be a float tube, but I have not done so yet. I am not afraid of snakes, and in fact, I like them. As a young boy, I kept snakes as pets and to learn about their habits. I even had a few rattlesnakes that I eventually set free or donated to a local zoo. Looking back, it was crazy that my father let me have rattlesnakes even though I was careful and had been taught by a local herpetologist how to handle them. Still, I learned a great deal about them during that time. I bring this topic up because in the spring and summer when the bass are very active in these ponds, so are the water snakes, and although I have not had a confirmed sighting of a western cottonmouth on the Sabinal, I have seen them on the Llano and Guadalupe, and there's something unnerving about wading or floating with moccasins, even for a snake-lover like me.

Beyond the ponds, the river changes, as do the fish and the fishing. The water runs quick and shallow in places, and the fish turn from largemouth bass to Guadalupes that like to live trout-like in plunge pools and pocket water. Where the river narrows and meanders through tangles of maple trees, the fishing is stealthy, and casting is impossible beyond very short roll-cast or bow casts. Farther downstream, the trees give way and the sun shines down upon undercut banks where Guads love to wait in ambush. During the hot summer months, I have come to this lower section to wet wade in the cool spring water, casting toward submerged rocks and undercut banks. I remember each fish I have ever caught, although I must admit the many small sunfish tend to blend together in one flowing memory of green-and-yellow iridescent happiness.

In autumn, as the trees turn golden and the hoppers explode with every streamside step, the Sabinal becomes even more intimate, quiet, and even lonely. Each year, the leaf-peepers come in droves to watch the maples flame red while missing everything else. I tend to avoid the river during those times, but if I do come to fish here, I still find a strange solitude among the masses. I've noticed that as I stand there casting loop after loop in the brisk autumn air the maples see me, but the people do not. They pass me by looking up or down and often never notice the man standing in the river. I am pleased by this and find myself in the good company of equally invisible deer, turkey, and porcupines.

After the leaves have fallen and transform from firelight red to earth-toned brown scattered along the trails and submerged beneath the shallow waters, I can still get a few good days of fishing in before the water turns cold. I walk along the river's edge, and if I see hoppers, I cast my imitations of the same. If I see mayflies coming off, I toss smaller bits of fur and feather. And, if nothing is hopping, floating, or flying, I swing streamers into the current hoping to entice a not-yet-too-sullen autumn bass.

When winter arrives in the Texas hills, the river becomes quiet. Still, I will go there and stand beneath the canyon's rim in cold, shallow water casting patiently, waiting . . . always waiting for something to happen. I slow down. I become more patient, just like the river. And then, when the trout arrive in their new home, the fishing picks up for a little while. They jump and dive at the end of my line and then slide from my hands back home once more. Like me, they were not born here, and their lives hang within an uncertain and all-too-fleeting season. It matters not. What matters is that we live truly within whatever season we are granted.

The Sabinal is timeless. I don't want to watch it fade away into the stone like a lost love walking into the sea. I don't want her to be alive only within my aging, fading memory. Even though the state has protected its headwaters within parkland, it can do nothing for its ever-more-rarified lifeblood. Geography saves it more than legality ever will. It lives nearly a hundred miles from the nearest city. Still, its shining, emerald fish, clay-colored deer, copperhead snakes, and golden-cheeked warblers are all connected to the aquifer below the rock, as is the distant city.

The canyon that is formed by the headwaters of the Sabinal River is a magical place for me. Only once did I see the mouflon ram and the many sheep of the herd that ran behind him. After all these years, he has not reappeared to me, although I know he is there. I have hiked these canyon lands for decades, always looking for the rare and endemic golden-cheeked warbler. Until this transformative year, I had never seen one. And then, one bright day, Megan and I were hiking past the ponds and I was speaking of a lifetime searching and, at that moment, he was there singing in the oak tree overhead. I see his image in my mind and hear his voice every time I pass that tree. Indeed, this place is inhabited by ghosts, and I see them drifting with the river when perhaps no one else can; they are, after all, my ghosts. Always, I am haunted by these waters.

Chapter Seven

Guadalupe

Sometimes, if you stand on the bottom rail of a bridge and lean over to watch the river slipping slowly away beneath you, you will suddenly know everything there is to be known.

~Winnie-the-Pooh

I HAVE OFTEN WONDERED WHICH WATER IS MY HOMEWATER. I HAVE wondered if it is the clear-running Llano, or perhaps the lovely little Medina, or the Sabinal as it runs out of the canyon toward the sea. And then, there is one more river that I must consider, the place where I have spent so many thoughtless hours casting and catching and, most of all, just being. It runs from the canyons above the town of Mountain Home through the ranchlands that surround the town of Comfort and onward toward Canyon Dam where it gathers itself, deep and cold, and where its tailwaters shelter rainbow and brown trout beneath the ancient cypress trees. Many soulless metallic exoskeletons cross the Guadalupe, and the soulless bodies within them never look down, hear her voice, or grow to love her as I love her.

There is a bridge that crosses the Guadalupe just over one of my favorite places to fish. There are many roads that cross her, but this bridge holds magic beneath it. There is a place beneath a pecan tree where I park and prepare, stringing up my rod as I listen to birdsong and the sound of wind in the grass, a sound that reflects my life. And then I walk over to this lonely bridge and keep it company. I lean over the rail and watch the river slip slowly beneath me. I hear the wren song coming from the canyon's edge and watch the kingfisher who is watching the river too. I smell the fresh rainwater smell rise up to me, and I see how the morning sunlight glistens off the water. It does not matter what burdens I carry . . . they too slip away like autumn leaves, like winter mist, like springtime blossoms, and like the sleek summer garter snake who fishes here also. I have spent a lifetime watching this river slip away from the bridge's top railing, and each time I do, I come to know all that ever needs to be known. I know peace.

These waters are my homewaters. This is where I taught Megan to fly-fish, or rather where she taught herself. We have fished the upstream and downstream of this place together. Sometimes I stop fishing and just watch her cast, breaking all the rules, sticking her backside out trying to get a few extra feet of distance, casting long loops gently upon the water.

One time I couldn't stop catching fish. Every cast brought a strike and bass after bass and sunfish after sunfish came to my hand, and Megan could not get a bite. I even tried to abandon the spot, walking away, not realizing that my streamer was trailing behind me until a bass latched on to it. So I cast toward a shallow, worthless spot beneath a cypress root and found a sunfish on the end of my line anyway. I felt bad since I always enjoy watching her catch fish even more than catching them myself. She caught me trying to hide the bright flapping fish with my leg as I slipped it off the hook and into the river. She said, "It's all right, Dad, I'm having fun no matter if I catch one or not . . . I'm here with you!"

Sometimes when she is away, I come here without her. The water is just as lovely. The birds sing just as sweetly. The fish jump just as high. But without her here to smile and laugh with, the river seems just a little darker, a little more silent, lonelier. Reflections bring beauty to a moment, and they can bring longing.

When I think of the Guadalupe, memories flood through my mind and over the rocks and into deep pools. I think of this spot beneath the bridge, the upstream and downstream character of it, and how it makes me feel. I think of deer and javelina running along its banks as I cast to the place behind the rock, or beneath the cypress root, or along the undercut riverbank I have come to know so well.

Being my homewater, I know its secret places, and it, I suspect, knows mine. I think of brightly colored map turtles and prehistoric-looking, softshell turtles swimming past my legs and of the banded water snakes and ribbon snakes that fish for minnows along the shore. And then there was the time I was casting into the deep limestone ridge that runs through the river's center and I saw a cottonmouth swimming in front of me with a live five-inch channel catfish in its mouth. It swam to shore where it waited until the fish stopped flapping and then ate it while I waded a little farther downriver. Once a year, the swallows come to nest beneath the bridge, and they swoop and soar overhead, making tighter aerial loops than I could ever muster.

Upstream of the bridge is a long run of shallow riffles. The river runs over prehistoric limestone that is cut in parallel waves from the endless action of the water as it runs from the canyon carving springs toward the sea. These same drops of water ultimately travel toward the sky only to fall once more from low-slung, western-sky clouds, seeping home into their limestone bed, again. Black Elk was right . . . everything in life is a circle.

Often, I wade through this expanse of fast-running riffles perhaps only six inches deep without casting, just looking, for holes. Rivers speak in metaphor, and holes contain both peril and promise of life. When the drought has come and the world seems to grow shallow, I think of holes. There are many kinds of holes in our lives. There are the literal holes that we can step into, fall into, and trip over if we are not careful. There are holes in our logic and our thinking in general. There might be holes in our faith, but we tend to fill those up with more faith. Then, there are the holes left inside us by the loss of someone we hold dear.

There are many ways to lose a loved one. Sometimes, it is forever, as in death, even if in our hearts they are with us always. Sometimes, it is for a moment or a day, but it feels like forever. When that happens, it is as Bryce Courtenay describes in his book *The Power of One*, "the loneliness bird lays stone eggs inside you." When you lose or feel that you lose your connection with someone you love, it feels hollow and empty, deep down . . . a cavern of silence where only the dripping of memories into the abyss keeps you company, and you reach for their hand but only touch the empty air. Empty. Hollow: that is how holes feel.

The trick with holes is not to stand at the edge of them. If you do, you will always find yourself looking down into the black and wishing they were not holes. It is better to turn about, to walk away with some courage intact, to tell yourself that it doesn't matter, that the hole can be filled—will be filled. It is better to remember the days when the hole was not there, to find a smile in those memories, and to tell the loneliness bird to go to hell.

There have been many holes in my life. When my Marine Corps brother Dave died, a piece of me died with him. I remember crying when they called to tell me he was gone. I remember crying when I sat in the back of the funeral home, frozen, unable to move forward. I remember how Dave's mother took my arm and spoke to me softly and how we walked so that I did not know we were walking, and then suddenly, I was at the casket, and she told me to look, and all I could see was the hole.

Sometimes when I walk along these shallow riffles, I look up through the holes in the clouds, and I imagine that I can see Dave looking down at me. Holes work both ways, I guess. In the end, if there is an end, this is the problem with love. If you are a watchful soul, you come to know that great love cannot exist without great joy and great pain. A coward will shun love to avoid the pain. A courageous and living spirit must walk the dark path and look to the stars. A courageous spirit does not avoid the pain because he cannot endure a life void of joy.

Sometimes when you are in a hole or the hole is in you, it is not because the person you love has died but rather because they are in a hole too. If this is the case, and you truly love them, there is only one thing that you can do. You must stand at the hole's edge, reach down into the darkness, and wait. In time, if you truly love them, and they truly love you, two hands will grasp in the darkness, and the darkness will become light, and you will embrace the one you love, and even if only for a moment in time, you will smile at each other and say, "It's you!" Holes have a way of filling up like that.

These upstream riffles contain holes. As the water grows thin with the summer heat, it is the holes that give refuge to the fish. If the river is running well, I will cast to them, catching a fish here and there and then releasing them quickly back into their sheltered hole. About a half mile upstream there is a long, deep pool that I have named the "bass-hole." I am always amazed at how many Guadalupes seem to call it home. If the river is shallow, I simply search with my eyes and not my line. I see the bass, sunfish, channel cats, and carp swimming deep within the darkness of the hole and I feel happy knowing that at least for now they are sheltered within its shaded depths.

Downstream there is an island where white-tailed deer like to sleep and water snakes like to hunt. At the bottom of the island, the river bends beneath the shade of giant cypress trees. I cast toward their grasping roots and the many boulders that rise from the river bottom into the warm Texas air. Sometimes I see the discarded exoskeletons of various caddis flies, damselflies, and dragonflies upon the sticks and stones. Sometimes I see the adults hovering gracefully overhead. There is a red-tailed hawk, my brother Dave's spirit animal, who is always there watching over me. In fact, he calls to me from the Guadalupe, the Llano, and Colorado Bend. He seems to be with me always, as a different bird perhaps, but still the same spirit.

There is a spot about a half mile downstream of my bridge where the river undercuts the bank deeply beneath the cypress trees. I have caught many bass and sunfish, a few channel cats, and, once, even a small fish I could not identify with a tetra-like face filled with tiny teeth. This curve in the river challenges me because it always contains the one fish I have never been able to catch: carp.

I see carp in many Texas Hill Country rivers: Llano, Frio, Nueces, San Marcos, and, of course, the Guadalupe. I have cast to them with woolly buggers and woolly worms, bitch creeks and prince nymphs, and anything I can think of using in my effort to hook one of these golden bottom feeders. I don't know why I care, perhaps because they look so much like freshwater bonefish or perhaps just because they have eluded me for so long. In other rivers, I find carp here and there cruising up and down the river. On the Guadalupe, I always find them here in this single bend in the river. I keep casting.

Just beyond the bend are a series of shallow, fast-running riffles and pocket water that gather beneath ancient trees and then tumble into a postcard pool. I hear the distant sound of longhorn cattle calling from the adjacent pasture. White-tailed deer jump from their beds at the river's edge, and a kingfisher patrols up and down the river overhead. I cast into the depths just below a massive boulder, and every now and then, I manage to connect to a nice-sized bass that carries this river's surname.

Walking back upstream I always take my time, not fishing, just being alive as I wade in a stretch of river where the water is a mere eight inches deep over the ancient limestone. The eons have worn the stone into the shapes of running water interrupted only by the occasional boulder or dinosaur track. These rivers hold history within.

The Guadalupe contains dinosaur tracks near Canyon Lake, and there are more along Cibolo Creek and in the bedrock of the Blanco. Not all that far from my bridge, there is a streambed at Government Canyon where Spanish moss sways in the oak trees, birds sing, side-blotched lizards dart, and the footprints of an Acrocanthosaurus dinosaur can be seen and felt. The last time I was there, the stream was dry, or rather it was hidden beneath the stone, and upon the stone, I sat next to the footprints of the Acrocanthosaurus.

If we pay attention, nature teaches us humility. It gives me perspective to know that over sixty-five million years ago this thirty-foot-long predator stepped in the mud of that stream and left its mark. The enormous beating heart it had is no longer, yet the impressions of its lifetime remain. I thought about how small our lives are within the space and time of this universe. Before leaving . . . I stepped in the mud next to the dinosaur tracks. Who knows?

———

I have fished my homewater many times over the years, most often from its headwaters downstream toward Sisterdale. One day in late spring, I decided to try the waters of Guadalupe River State Park. I have hiked and even mountain-biked its trails many times but had never fished it. I had even kayaked a stretch just below the park, but I was paddling that day, not casting. Megan went with me on that trip, and when we got to a section of small rapids that ran down and around some fallen trees, I asked her what she thought about running that aquatic obstacle course, to which she answered, "Cool!" She is so very much her dad's kid, even now that she's all grown up. Like me, Megan loves adventure.

Like me, my daughter has been on a journey of self-invention or, more accurately, self-revelation. While I find myself looking at a lifetime that almost seems to belong to another being, and now choosing a path that will be truer to my true self and what I have learned about the world, she finds herself like so many thoughtful young people in these times wondering what path to take? In truth, and in fact, we are traveling the same journey, Megan and me. The only difference is that she is just beginning, and I have a lot more mileage on my face and my soul and many fewer heartbeats remaining.

Martin Shaw once wrote, "To be in touch with wilderness is to have stepped past the proud cattle of the field and wandered far from the twinkles of the Inn's fire. To have sensed something sublime in the life/death/life movement of the seasons, to know that contained in you is the knowledge to pull the sword from the stone and to live well in fierce woods in deep winter." These words speak to me. Even as a boy, I have always been a wild man. I never could endure being locked indoors, and nothing has changed. It doesn't matter if I am climbing mountains in Peru, Italy, or Montana, or if I am rolling off the gunnel of a boat into the seas of the Caribbean or carrying a rifle through the tall grass of Africa or casting a fly line into a Texas Hill Country river, I must be in the wild in order to feel free. And now I am here at my writing desk wishing it was outside somehow and dreaming of the next adventure.

Sometimes the universe is screaming at us, if only we take the time to listen. Things do seem to happen for a reason, or perhaps more correctly, we can discover the meaning within anything that may happen. The pause between Megan's undergraduate and graduate degrees allowed us to share this wonderful adventure together and allowed her the time to listen to her inner voice. This time of fishing and hiking with her dad allowed her to realize her desire for an outdoor life, and in doing so, she found her life path. She chose to combine her love of the outdoors with her love of teaching, service, and writing. Megan discovered that she, like me, needs to regularly be in the wild and natural spaces in order to live a meaningful life. Nature saves us. Nature teaches us. Nature heals us.

As for me, I am finding my way too. I am teaching college students part-time, trying to expand minds more than impart "knowledge," and I always learn as I teach. I am writing, healing, and reinventing life while hiking and fly-fishing the Texas Hill Country. One thing is certain, with each passing day as I get closer to the end of this mortal journey, I intend and insist on regaining my inner wilderness and with it my freedom.

On this day, I was alone but not lonely. I drove into Guadalupe River State Park along the winding road toward the river, passing white-tailed deer and bluebirds, live oaks and mountain cedars. I strung up my rod and tied on one of the best streamers anyone can use in these rivers, an olive woolly bugger with rainbow Krystal flash. If there is a second-best streamer, or perhaps tied for first best, it is the chartreuse and white Clouser Deep Minnow. Either of these streamers cast down and across are deadly on each type of bass these rivers hold: Guadalupe, largemouth, smallmouth, spotted, and, unfortunately, hybrid Guadalupe/smallmouth bass.

After a short walk along a riverside path, I found a place to enter where the water was running fast into a narrow shoot that was created by park rangers who stacked rocks so that they formed a funnel. This was the last sign of humanity I would see on this trip . . . almost.

This is one of those places where you must stop fishing from time to time and just look around you. After the ranger-made rock funnel, there is nothing except the river and the feeling of wilderness. I cast a few times toward the semi-submerged roots of cypress trees that have trunks half a dozen feet thick at the base. They tower over me in a primeval canopy of transient leaves.

A red-tailed hawk calls overhead, but I cannot see him. Wrens, warblers, cardinals, and titmice sing in the thick brush. I cast again and find myself attached to a slab-sided yellow-bellied sunfish that puts up a valiant fight before coming to hand and being released. I thank him. I cast again, and this time a small Guadalupe bass leaps into the air. He is emerald-green and studded with olive-green dashes across his belly. I release him, and as I do, I stop to ponder the wildness of this spot.

I listen to the sound of the river running over rock and the birds floating on the air and the wind speaking to the leaves. I smell the organic aroma of life and the freshness of the air that touches my timeworn skin. I feel the pulling of the water against my legs and my heart, my heart that beats almost to the same rhythm as the river. Everywhere around me is the look and feel of wilderness, of a world untouched, of truth. And then I hear thunder that is not thunder, and I look up through the primeval treetops and watch as an Air Force fighter jet roars across the riverbank, and in that instant, the spell is broken until the jet passes.

When the interloper is gone, I am surrounded by the sound of unseen coyotes calling from the riverbank. They call the wilderness back to me. I understand why they call out, asking, "Is anyone out there?" They assure themselves that they are not alone, like we do, when we see ourselves in a painting, a work of prose, or a poem. At that moment, as the image comes to us through our eyes and our minds into our souls, we understand that we are not alone in the wilderness and that someone else is calling out too. I cast once more.

—⸺—

The summer is almost over, even if the hottest days are here. This summer has not been as hot as the last, where forty-eight days in a row the temperature topped one hundred degrees, but the drought has gotten worse, and everything suffers without the water that some of us need to drink and others need to breathe. I need water to drink and bathe just as any other human, but I find that more and more with each passing day I need the clear waters of these Texas Hills or some distant Caribbean sand flat just so I can continue to breathe.

I recently found a quote by a man who goes by the name Hans Hoffman. Hans said, "The ability to simplify means to eliminate the unnecessary so that the necessary may speak." This is a simple truth, I feel.

His words reach out to me each day. If I were a nation and that nation had a flag, it would most likely be a blue field with no other markings, eliminating the unnecessary, declaring, "This is me, I am the sea and the sky, and the deep pool where the cutthroat trout lives sipping mayflies." Nature is simple in its complexity; it is honest in both its cruelty and kindness. Each moment is just as it is and nothing else. Only the human mind builds entanglements and pretense. Turtle shells come as they do, covered in algae or covered in color.

Things were beginning to feel complicated lately, and that is when I knew it was time to get centered. When I begin to feel that tightness deep in my chest and the demons of the past come to call in my night dreams, it is then that I know I must go to the healing place; I must go to the river.

Today, Megan and I explored the headwaters of the Guadalupe. We stood in cool, clear water on a warm Texas day casting to fish that live at the base of a waterfall. Neon-blue dragonflies hovered near, and a beautiful checkered garter snake swam beneath the river's surface at my approach. Cypress trees shaded us from the sun, and everyone we met was a Texan; everyone was polite, kind, and respectful.

When I'm casting my line into the clear waters of the Texas Hills . . . life is simple once more . . . and simplicity is truth. Sometimes the most honest thing we can do in life is just sit in a rocking chair with our boots up on the rail watching the sunset over the hills. Simplicity, simplicity, simplicity . . . life!

I like the following quote from Tom Robbins's book *Still Life with Woodpecker*: "We are our own dragons as well as our own heroes, and we have to rescue ourselves from ourselves." This is true for me and I suspect for most people of good conscience that we put expectations upon ourselves and our lives and, in doing so, cause our inner peace to be robbed from us.

When your spirit feels homeless, there is nothing quite as powerful as the magic of homewater. Recently, I had the pleasure of reading a book by an author whom every angler with an ounce of soul should get to know. In her book *The View from Coal Creek*, Erin Block speaks of homewater in a way that spoke to me. She wrote, "Homewater counts, for the secrets told, and the familiar skin. They hold the stories, and the histories of sea-son upon season, piled up like autumn leaves over the winter, keeping you warm and the fires going." I wish I wrote that. I'm grateful that she did.

Sometimes, thinking is bad for you. Recently, I knew I'd begun "thinking" too much. I have felt very quiet inside, like the moment after a battle when all the dust is settling upon the land and the wind blows through the trees and the one soldier left on the battlefield just sits there, alone, breathing, and taking time to notice how beautiful the sky is and the way the grass bends in the wind. That is me as each day is born and turns to sleep. Each day, not knowing what comes next, I simply continue to cast.

Megan and I drove west toward the "cowboy capital" town of Ban-dera for a morning breakfast at the local café. We sat by the window over-looking Main Street where pickup trucks and the occasional happy soul on horseback go by and where the window boxes are filled with flowering succulents. It's a nice place to just be, sip coffee, and wake up before a day fishing or hiking in the canyons.

On the limestone walls are photos of the Texas Hills and an old map of The Republic of Texas. The tables and chairs are made of Mexican mesquite and leather. Everything from the stamped-tin ceiling to the smiles of the pretty girls looks very Texan. Near the register are bills of currency from all around the world, including a few from prewar Iraq with the face of Saddam Hussein upon them. As I looked upon that wall, I noticed all the currency from places I've been and those I have not. I noticed how many of those nations depicted have fallen or the currency has changed. Impermanence is perpetual.

We left the café saying "adios" to the girls behind the counter and then crossed Main Street toward where we had parked, near the Arkey Blue's Silver Dollar Saloon. After forty-five years, Mr. Arkey Blue still owns this tiny Texas honky-tonk where legends like Ernest Tubb, Willie Nelson, and Hank Williams Jr. have all played. But on this morning, only the sound of silence came from its open door. Honky-tonks sleep in the daytime, I guess.

We drove north toward Kerrville, passing a herd of bison that were grazing just across from Camp Verde. Way back before the War Between the States, this was a camel depot where the military tested to see if a herd of one-humpers might work well for crossing the Texas deserts. The Secretary of War Jefferson Davis sent Colonel Robert Edward Lee to oversee the experiment. There is a cabin very close to my house where Lee stayed while preparing to go to Camp Verde and then, ultimately, on to Fort Davis to fight Comanche and Lipan Apache war parties.

These hills are full of ghosts, and as we drove north along Verde Creek, I thought about how I was seeing the same hills and perhaps some of the same old trees that shaded Lee, Jeb Stuart, and the Comanche war parties. I can envision the horses and riders crossing the field that now contains bison behind a high fence. Sometimes in my visions, they wear the accoutrements of plains natives, and other times I can see the single star of a Texas banner fluttering as Captain Hays rides with his Rangers to meet Buffalo Hump and his braves at the Battle of Bandera Pass. In 1841, this battle pitted fifty Texas Rangers with Colt repeating pistols against several hundred braves of the Penateka band of Comanche's. The Rangers held off the attack throughout the day.

Ultimately, Colonel Hays and Chief Buffalo Hump would become admirers of each other's actions, and at the birth of the Ranger's first child, the Comanche chief sent a gift in his honor. All landscapes are historical landscapes, and the hands of former lives shape them as surely as do the raindrops and the rivers. These hills are full of ghosts.

We were traveling toward the headwaters of my home river, though oddly enough, I had never fished them or even laid eyes upon them until this day. We followed the Guadalupe into Kerrville, through Ingram and onward to Hunt, where the north and south forks of the Guadalupe merge. I kept driving until near Hunt the river grew small and shallow yet full of promise and the feeling of wilderness.

It always amazes me how a shallow, winding stream can have above it the towering sheer limestone cliffs that it created over the eons. Arroyos run dry or full depending upon the season, and in each instance, the power of rainwater can be seen and felt. This land is carved by water just as my face has been creased by wind, sunlight, time, and laughter.

Megan and I were practicing that kind of leisurely fishing that John Gierach once described as "fishing along at about the same pace that an archeologist sifts dirt, taking all the time in the world so as not to miss anything." We jumped from river crossing to crossing west of Hunt, taking time to enjoy the sound of birds and the explosive jumping of frogs and the gentle white noise of falling water. We cast to dozens of nice bass in the one- to two-pound range, and although she got a vicious strike but lost the fish, all I caught were rays of sunshine and an overhanging tree limb. It mattered not, we were exploring, and I knew that these headwaters were magical, and I was even a little ashamed that I had not come here sooner.

In time, we came to a crossing that held the name "Dry Crossing." It was. We had followed my homewater as far as we could, but I could still see where it traveled beneath the rocky ground-scape and the way it creased the hills.

Looking out over the hills scattered with oak trees and cedar, the prickly pears standing dry along the birthplace of the Guadalupe, I think of how she winds and runs over so much of Texas. I think of her deep, cool canyons and fast runs and how far from this spot this little river spills into the Gulf of Mexico where redfish feed in the grassy bays. Where is her home . . . in these dry hills or in that vast sea? I think, like me, this is her homewater. This place is the place where we both return and where we are reborn.

<hr>

Sometimes as I look out upon these Texas hills or stand in the fast, clear streams that I call home, I feel the same sense of trepidation that parents have for their children, knowing that life will leave its scars upon them and wishing there was some way to spare them of this eventuality. I am a Texan, through and through, deep in my heart . . . but like Davy Crocket, Jim Bowie, Sam Houston, and Stephen Austin, I wasn't born here. I grew up on the edge of the Florida Everglades before the circus came to town and the invasion from the north and south destroyed a landscape and its culture.

As a child, my homewater was the Loxahatchee River and the saw-grass flats of Okeechobee. Back then, I cast my line into tea-stained waters for black bass and bluegills to the sound of gators bellowing and panthers screaming. Now, all of this is gone. Now, all this is altered, forever.

What once were islands of humanity surrounded by a sea of wilderness is the reverse, and the rare pocket-water wilderness not yet touched by "progress" has still been infected by feral pythons and mercury-tainted water. So, as I look out at the still-clean, clear, undeveloped canyon waters of my beloved Texas hills, I fear for her.

I have learned that no one loves that which they do not know and that only love can protect anything. I have learned that this world runs on power, and the bloodstream of power is flowing with money and even love can't seem to stop the bleeding once it starts. I fear for this landscape and our Hill Country culture, and I write these words hoping to cause others to love this rare place but love it enough to let it be. I wish to live here in this place and fish my homewater until I live no more. Still, if the circus comes to town and she is lost, I would rather leave and remember her as she once was . . . lovely, wild, and free.

I am often reminded of what truly matters by the words left behind by others . . . words that act as artifacts from ancient oracles. These words travel through time, outliving their origins. D. H. Lawrence once wrote, "What we want is to destroy our false, inorganic connections, especially those related to money, and re-establish the living organic connections, with the cosmos, the sun and earth, with mankind and nation and family. Start with the sun, and the rest will slowly, slowly happen." And I do, in fact, want to peel off each layer of the unnecessary and work life down to the bone and marrow of it all. So, I return to my homewaters and stand on the bottom rail of a bridge and lean over to watch the river slipping slowly away beneath me, and suddenly, I know everything there is to be known . . . I know peace.

Chapter Eight

West Verde Creek

The individual has always had to struggle to keep from being over-whelmed by the tribe. If you try it, you will be lonely often, and sometimes frightened. But no price is too high to pay for the privilege of owning yourself.

~ *Friedrich Nietzsche*

By the time I arrived at Verde Creek, it was gone ... or at least nearly so. I had done some research on the creek and read that it was a thriving Hill Country spring creek with good populations of native Guadalupe bass and yellow-bellied sunfish living in the quick water that tumbles over limestone. I also knew that there were several tanks that contained native largemouth bass and bluegill. It was the running water and the Guadalupes that interested me. I found a photo of a fly fisherman standing in the West Verde playing a leaping Guadalupe bass in a plunge pool at the base of a small waterfall. I knew then that I wanted to be that guy, and so I planned a combined fly-fishing and hiking expedition to Hill Country Natural Area State Park, where the West Verde Creek flows entirely within its borders.

The problem with being a river is that once you spill yourself out for the good of every tree and blade of grass there is nothing left of you to tumble over the rocks. Still, it's a good thing to be a river, if it rains from time to time. This is how I see this moment in my life and how it is reflected in this little spring creek that is dying. We need rain . . . yes, but more than that, we need to stop bleeding life so everyone else can drink. We need to practice resilience and be allowed time to recover, and in doing so, the trees and grasses and distant spigots, metallic or human, may need to go elsewhere for a while when seeking their redemption.

I found West Verde Creek just inside the entrance of the park. It was surrounded by some of the most beautiful hills I have seen in this country. Along the hillsides, fields of sotol bloomed, their flowering spires pointing toward the sky. Live oak, red oak, and mountain cedar covered the hilltops while pecan, hickory, walnut, and mesquite dominated the bottomlands.

I parked at the stream crossing and gazed into the few small pools that remained in a mostly dry creek. Small sunfish swam in ever-tightening circles as their "sky" continued to fall. Just beyond the crossing, I saw the spot where the happy fly fisherman had been playing the Guadalupe bass in the plunge pool. The falls were now only naked, dry limestone and the plunge pool had become a stagnant circle of desperation for the few tiny sunfish still living in that ever-shrinking world. Prospecting along the creek, I found other pools of trapped fish, and even if I could, I decided I would never add to their plight by casting a line of hopelessness toward them. I wished I had real mayflies to offer them.

When I went into the park ranger's office to check-in and show my park pass, I asked about West Verde Creek. Behind the desk was a petite young woman in a park service uniform. Her smile briefly evaporated, much like the remaining creek. She said, "It's sad, the springs stopped flowing this year for the first time I can remember. We'll need a lot of rain to get them flowing again." She confirmed that they hadn't seen any Guadalupe bass in the creek for some time and that only a few yellow-bellied sunfish remain in the occasional pools.

What spells doom for the fish is a feast for herons and raccoons. I knew even as she spoke, we needed much more than rain showers. While it is true that the Hill Country and most of Texas has experienced a prolonged period of extreme drought, it is also true that this park and its springs are fed by the Edwards Aquifer, the same aquifer that feeds San Antonio with water for drinking, irrigation, waste disposal, and recreation. I knew the truth was closer to what Edward Abbey wrote in his classic book *Desert Solitaire*: "There is no lack of water here, unless you try to establish a city where no city should be."

I think it's true that any trip on which you take a fly rod with the intention of fishing is a fishing trip. It doesn't matter if you cast your line or catch a fish; what matters is your honest intention to do both or either. In this case, I could have cast toward those sad sunfish, but that would have been a sin. Instead, I decided to keep a clear conscience and not tarnish my soul any more than needed. My fly rod stayed in its case, and I went hiking into the hills that have looked over West Verde Creek for eons.

The landscape here is stunning. The Texas Hill Country isn't the kind of over-the-top beauty that I have seen in the Rocky Mountains; it is subtler than that . . . you must pay attention. Each step brings new vistas, both distant and near, macro- and micro-universes, which live here. Sometimes I experience this by walking or casting as I move methodically forward uphill or downhill . . . upstream or downstream. Often, it is during those times that I stop walking or stop casting and I take a moment to just pay attention. Mindfulness is a way of being that we are losing touch with in America, and fly-fishing or walking mindfully is as much a meditative practice as sitting in a temple staring at the wall can ever be.

The hills around West Verde Creek are a wonderful place to pay attention. At the trailhead, there is a sign warning of rattlesnakes. A few steps down the trailhead, I saw a cottontail rabbit beneath a cedar tree. Cottontails are not that common here, but I do see them from time to time along with the much larger jackrabbits. In either case, it must be tough being born to a life serving as a basic staple in the food chain. This little guy was only yards away from the rattlesnake warning sign, and around it were coyote tracks, and above it was a red-tailed hawk. Nature is often beautiful, always wondrous, and rarely kind. There is no path to self-actualization for a bunny.

Just beyond the cottontail, I found a small patch of prairie paintbrush. The fire-red Indian paintbrush is common in these hills, but until that moment, I had never seen the multicolored prairie variety. As in each landscape, elevation and soil, or lack thereof, are the keys to flora and fauna. As I climbed higher up into the hills, the hickory, pecan, redbud, and mesquite turned to mountain cedar and oak.

Green anoles were replaced by spiny lizards and red-winged blackbirds by warblers, chickadees, and black-crested titmice. It was spring, and the wildflowers covered the earth from the edge of the creek bed to the caliche-sided hills. The sotol were in full bloom. Looking across the canyon, I could see endless spires reaching toward the sky, each one hopeful, searching, continuing the existence of its kind.

For a while, I chose to just stand there on the hillside, looking across the canyon, not thinking, just being. Across the bottom of the canyon, I saw the line of cypress and pecan trees that wind along West Verde Creek. They, too, count on its spring waters to return. I wondered if they ever would. If they do not, will this landscape change irrevocably? How can we let this happen? Climbing to the overlook, I could see what seemed like endless hills in the distance. I knew that they are not endless and that each living thing is lost, one thoughtless act at a time.

I began my descent through the hills, and in time, the landscape changed again to grassy meadows mixed with mesquite. It was then that I heard the loud warning grunt of a big wild boar. I stopped and looked intently beneath the branches and chest-high grass. It was then that I saw about eight to ten wild hogs with a big boar hog on guard. He was staring at me as I stared back at him. He didn't seem friendly. I did not have my pistol in my pack, so if he charged, I could only hurl insults at him and climb a tree. Looking around, I found no suitable trees, so the insults would have to do. I moved out of his territory while keeping a wary eye on him.

The sun was high overhead, and the day was getting warm. At the trailhead, there were a few people camping with their horses. I saw one group riding their horse through the hills on the trail as well. I stood aside so they could pass, and we greeted each other in pure Texan fashion . . . you know, sincerely. There was a man about ten years my senior and a woman much younger than he, perhaps his daughter. She smiled and said hello from atop a beautiful horse with black-and-white patches and a blazed forehead. He tipped his hat, and for a moment, as the horses picked their way down the rocky trail, we spoke of the amazing sunlight in these hills and the need to watch out for rattlers.

At the trailhead, I decided to sit and breathe in the fresh air of that beautiful day. There were a few picnic benches under live oak trees, and it was nice to watch the large spiny lizards hunting among each twisted trunk. The breeze cooled the air in a way that made the sunlit warmth on my cheek feel like something to revel in and recall. I could see West Verde Creek just beyond the flower-studded meadow. Texas paintbrush, fire-wheel, and Mexican hat blooms lined the trail. The breeze moved the meadow grasses in waves, not in unison. The landscape was alive. A chickadee watched me from above and chirped at me; it was either a greeting or a scolding—I wasn't sure. This was a good place to sit and not think too much. This was a good place to simply be, mindful, in-the-moment, alive.

It has been a rough decade for me, but that's life. The sun comes up and sets and the stars come out. Flowers bloom and fade. Fairness is a silly notion. Mayflies have a single day to live a lifetime; they need to make the most of it. Over a career of more than twenty years, I did what I thought I should do, and that's okay. I worked hard and, in my own small way, made some small difference. Sitting and looking across the meadow at the mostly dry creek, I knew something had changed. Looking at the remains of West Verde Creek was like looking in the mirror and noticing how deep the lines are cut: scar overlapping scar.

Civilization is like a rattler; you should never get too close. It has a way of making you spill out all over the place until there's nothing left. Society tells each of us that it's for your own good . . . but that is a lie, and we each must know when to walk away. Sometimes, maybe most of the time, we must provide our own rain. It's a constant balance between not letting too much of yourself be lost among the rocks and remembering to replenish what is lost. Sometimes, the bravest thing you can do is walk away.

We each live off the fruits of our decisions and indecisions; I am no exception to this rule. The rabbit turns left and finds clover; he turns right and finds a hawk. Such is life and death. Still, it's important that we choose which way we turn. Sometimes, maybe most of the time, doing what your heart tells you to do leads down a lonely path. Like attracts like. Most people shun the nonconformist. It matters not. No price is too high to pay for authentic living. We are all mayflies living our own brief day. If nothing else, I have learned to live urgently. Life's not a dress rehearsal. There are no "do-overs."

If I'm honest about it, I guess I'm weird. I don't treat wildlife or wildflowers as if their lives have any less value than mine. In each of those tiny sunfish beats a heart, and somewhere within, whatever animates their lives is the will to keep on living.

I know that many people who do not hunt or fish and who identify themselves as "animal lovers" will never understand how someone can kill that which they love. Often, these same people, upon closer inspection, are the ones talking loudly and looking at their feet as they walk a park trail, or even more likely, they never actually get outdoors in wild nature. Their idea of nature is what they see on cable television. They call themselves animal lovers because they "own" a dog or cat. (Anyone who has ever lived with a cat knows that the cat owns you.) I wish these well-meaning "animal lovers" and "preservationists" could come down out of the clouds and join the ranks of us ethical hunters and fishers. We are participants, not observers in nature. We take responsibility for the food we eat. It does not matter if the living thing is a carrot or a cow, something gives its life so that something else can live . . . it is the way of nature.

The only way to preserve nature and landscape is to remove all the people. We destroy as we go . . . it's our nature. We alter the landscape and cultivate plants, husband animals, harvest deer, and in the end, the only variable about humans is how deep our footprint is. This fact is why I say that I am a conservationist, not a preservationist. I focus on what might be possible, given current reality. I want to find ways to lessen the depth of our footprint.

Preservation may indeed someday come to pass. The question is, will we destroy the Earth at the same rate that we destroy ourselves, or will the Earth rebound? Recently, I was looking at a series of amazing photographs of endangered Ecuadorian rainforest frogs. Some of these photos were of the single, last-known living example of each species, male or female, each without any hope of a mate, each staring into eternal oblivion. As a naturalist who has visited the rainforests and cloud forests of South America, it moved me deeply.

I know that global greed for increased consumption of petroleum energy is driving the destruction of the Ecuadorian forests and its native people. As a naturalist, I also know that amphibians are the true "canaries in the coal mine" of our ecosystems. One thing that tells me that most of the Texas Hill Country is still "clean" is the proliferation of frogs in our spring-fed streams. Still, I see the concrete creeping north from San Antonio and west from Austin into the Hill Country, and the demand for water is ever increasing. When I see these photos, I am very aware that we are looking at the last images of these species. How sad. How sinful. How dare we?

The answer most likely lies in the outcome of the Fermi paradox, a concept to which my daughter introduced me. The Fermi paradox is an attempt to answer the question, "Where is everybody?" As we look toward the stars, we realize that there is a contradiction between the high mathematical probability of the existence of extraterrestrial civilizations and humanity's lack of known contact with, or evidence for, the existence of such civilizations. The Fermi paradox tries to answer why the Earth hasn't been colonized or visited by any other advanced life forms and why even though we can currently observe over eighty billion other galaxies in the known universe no convincing evidence has been detected that anyone else is out there.

Some scientists pondering this dilemma have concluded that the answer might be that they were once "out there" but that it is the nature of intelligent life to destroy itself. The argument is that perhaps we are on the same path they took toward self-annihilation via nuclear war, biological warfare, self-induced climate change, or something referred to as the Malthusian catastrophe or Malthusian check where the destruction of the Earth's ecosphere leads to massive population die-off as resources are exhausted.

Everything we do is a delaying action. Medical science only delays the inevitable. Conservation efforts only delay the same inevitable outcome as human populations increase. And, eventually, our solitary star that now keeps our planet alive will engulf it. Still, I'm in no rush. Let the stars hang as long as they may, and let's not foul our nest too quickly. There are too many people in the world, and we are unable or unwilling to balance the cause of liberty with self-regulating maturity. At some point, we will deal with this; I think it will be an effect rather than a cause.

When I lived in the Ivory Coast, I heard an Ivorian proverb that spoke of an elephant that rode on the back of a tortoise: "So that power never travels faster than wisdom allows." I suspect that our brains and our opposable thumbs have overshot our maturity. Like in the book and film *Jurassic Park*, we have spent so much time asking if we *could*, we forgot to ask if we *should*.

My father used to say, "We are only a single step outside of the cave." It's true when you think about it. We haven't changed anything about human nature. We have only traded our spears for intercontinental ballistic missiles tipped with nuclear warheads. I, for one, do not want to live in a world where frogs don't sing in the spring-night air. I'd rather have frogs hopping in the wetlands than hip-hop popping on the radio. There's something we once knew back in the days of the cave that we seem to have forgotten.

The truth is, I have a soft spot for small unknown creeks and streams. I'm still planning to return to West Verde Creek and stand where the water once spilled over the rocks and into the plunge pool. I want to see the native Guadalupe Bass return to this lovely spring creek. I'm not sure how we will save these waters from our own greed . . . perhaps the words I write are a start. We only save those things we come to love. We only love the things we come to know.

I remain optimistic. The West Verde isn't half empty, it's half full, or maybe, more importantly, it can be refilled. I fell in love with it, even in its dark moments, and if I can write anything here to help others love it too, then maybe together we can help it live. When that day comes, and the springs flow once more, I will cast my line into that pool, connecting to an emerald-and-onyx shadow. The shadow is only a shadow now, a reflection of what once was. Then, it will contain a beating heart complete with double-helix instructions for the future. And when I set him free once more into West Verde Creek and he swims away, we will both be home.

CHAPTER NINE

San Marcos

Uncertainty is an essential ingredient of adventure.
-- CHARLES CRAVER

THERE ARE A FEW THINGS I KNEW ABOUT THE SAN MARCOS RIVER. FOR example, I knew that its origin was the air-clear waters of Aquarena Springs, in Hays County, Texas. I could see the springs from the edge of the green space not far from the office where I had worked until the third round of budget cuts ended over three years of hard effort. While I was working in San Marcos, I had taken a glass-bottom boat trip across the surface of the springs, watching aquatic vegetation sway as turtles, bass, sunfish, and garfish swam beneath us. I saw the powerful jetting vents where the Edwards Aquifer brings the river to life with pure, clear water from deep within the limestone. I knew that the water of the San Marcos was amazingly clear, at least for the first mile or so, and that some of the rarest species of plants and animals in the world live here and only here, at least for now. The last thing I had learned about the San Marcos River is of the kayakers who had drowned beneath its currents. Of all the things

I knew, this would turn out to be the most prophetic. Uncertainty truly is the key ingredient of adventure.

We carried our kayaks to the river's edge where fast, clear water fell over a small dam and began its winding trail between the trees. The location was not too far from the center of the college town of San Marcos, and this was self-evident when I saw the trash cans chained to the tree that was covered in poison ivy, the beer cans in said trash can, the fire ring near the shoreline, and a girl's panties abandoned, wet and lonely, on the rocks. Her parents must be so proud.

I knew that this would be a part of the story of the river; college-aged irresponsibility and drunken behavior on both ends with wilderness in the middle. This is a story that must be told . . . the story of how we treat our national treasures and what we need to do about it. Still, on this morning, we had the river to ourselves, Megan and me. The birds sang in the treetops, turtles and water snakes basked on half-submerged tree bottoms, and fish leaped into the air catching damselflies. We secured our rods in the kayaks after tying on a couple of black woolly buggers and launched into the river.

Maps, no matter how well designed, do not do justice to the reality of the landscape. Even in the mountains I have found that the nearness of wavy lines on a topographical image gave only a hint to the character of any land. It may tell you that this area is flat and that the area is steep, but it hides from you the reality of the place. Maps never tell of the rocks filled with rattlers or that tangle of downed trees. They make no mention of the perfume of flowers or the sound of the water deep down in the canyons. Maps are devoid of wren song. This map told us that the next three miles would be a twisting, turning, narrow river and that when it began to twist and turn a bit less, this river, the San Marcos, would join that river, the Blanco. As we turned the corner, we began experiencing the limitations of maps.

The current was quick in most places, the river pulling us forward over submerged logs and under fallen trees. Turtles of every size lined the shoreline wherever there was an opening or where a fallen tree stump protruded from the water's surface. Here, just three miles down from the springs, the San Marcos is not the transparent river that I saw at its source. Instead, the water holds that crushed jade color that I have seen on the San Saba, as if somewhere deep behind us a temple might exist where monks spill the dust of gemstones into the river. Occasionally, I saw a turtle or some kind of large, dark, fish-like shadow just below the surface, but in most places, the bottom was not visible.

John Gierach once wrote a story in which he and a fishing buddy were discussing what might constitute a "fishing trip" and what did not. They concluded that it was a valid fishing trip if you go to the river with the intention to fish and have a fly-rod with you at the time. There would be fishing on this trip, but for the first many miles, there was nowhere to stand, no shoreline that wasn't covered in trees and poison ivy, no chance of resisting the current that pulled our kayaks and us ever forward. Still, as my 5 weight was by my side and Megan's 6 weight rested along the length of her kayak, it was already a "fishing trip."

The San Marcos is just barely able to qualify as a Hill Country river. At its source at Aquarena Springs, water as clear as mountain air gushes from the base of the very last hill before the land flattens out into the mixed woods and grasslands of the Central Texas Plains. The springs at its headwaters run strong, and so the river runs just as strong with many small rapids and some that are not so small that can, in fact, be life-threatening.

For the next three miles, we paddled, not so much to move forward in the quick current as to control our movement. The river corkscrewed between and under the thick, green, vegetative wall that encapsulates it in these few winding miles. The San Marcos is the only Texas Hill Country river that I have experienced where the trees that line its first few miles are principally massive, old box elder trees. Farther downriver, we started to see the cypress trees that I am used to seeing along the rivers and streams of the Edwards Plateau, but as we paddled through these first three to four miles, it felt more like the Congo than the Hill Country. I kept a wary eye out for cannibals.

We had the river to ourselves at this point . . . that is, if you don't count the flotilla of turtles either basking on logs or swimming beneath our kayaks along with dozens of frogs, a myriad of birds, and the occasional water snake. Fallen trees, a mixture of huge box elders and equally large sycamores, crossed the narrow winding river. We had to stay alert to find ways to "limbo" beneath them or paddle over them, sometimes maneuvering the kayaks in fast water between the branches of a fallen tree. Many times, I saw the shadows of massive unknown varieties of fish, but the current was strong, and for now, there would be no fishing on this fishing trip. We paddled and paddled until the heat began to rise and our arms grew weary.

After three or so miles of such paddling through rapids and rain-forest-like tangles, Megan called out, "It's like the African Queen . . . all we need are some leeches!" We both laughed, then we paddled onward . . . "down the river we go." Occasionally, the river slowed to a less frantic pace for no apparent reason than the way it turned and widened between the trees. At these moments, we rested our arms a bit until such time as I would hear rushing water, and like Bogie and Hepburn, we would brace ourselves and prepare to run the rapids over root and rock with our fly-rods suspended helplessly along our sides.

Even with all the effort, the sweat-dripping, arm-aching, out-of-breath, suspended-animation, time-stopping run around hairpin corners, under fallen trees, and over rushing water, the river was beautiful and as alive as we felt. I never knew what to expect with each bend or winding double back. The river extended in front of us, serpentine in nature, and it enclosed us within its primeval magic.

A small, banded water snake swam along the shore, then with the next turn came the watchful eyes of a night heron. Farther down, an osprey called from the treetops, as redbirds sang nearby. Always there was the sound of turtles sliding into the water at our approach. At one point, as I had just navigated a tight bend between a fallen sycamore and a standing cypress, Megan called out, "What kind of snake is that?" I spun my kayak to face her and saw immediately that I had just passed within two feet of what looked like a massive cottonmouth that was resting, curled up at the base of the cypress. He was beautiful in his coffee-colored camouflage.

And then the river widened, slowed, and the thick, jungle-like air became fresh, cooler, and welcoming. It was truly like the scene where Bogie and Hepburn reach the open water of the lake and can finally breathe deep, luxurious breaths. We unfurled our fly-rods and began casting along the banks. The wind and the current made casting while drifting a difficult and inelegant affair. The water here was deep and dark, and every so often, I saw the shadow of some massive fish just off the bow of my kayak.

I cast several times toward the shadow, not knowing what it was, and then feeling somewhat relieved that it didn't take the fly. Had I been in the Everglades or even East Texas, I might have concluded that it was a bowfin, but ancient bowfin fish are not supposed to be in these waters, and so to this day, I have no idea what I was seeing. I saw similar shadows once in a deep pool on the Llano River . . . catfish, perhaps? No, the shadows were the wrong shape for either catfish or garfish. Could it be a prehistoric monster fish? I decided to keep my legs inside the kayak's hull.

With the wind whipping and prehistoric shadows drifting below us, we decided to reel in and begin paddling downriver once again. The river was wide here, perhaps a hundred yards, whereas it may have been only fifteen feet wide in the areas where we were running the rapids. But here and now, it had taken on yet another personality. At its source, it is so clear that it feels as if you are looking into a well-kept aquarium. Then as the river narrows and quickens, it turns into crushed jade. Here, it was deep and dark and slightly lazy. The box elder trees gave way to the more familiar bald cypress, and for the first time, we could rest our arms a bit and enjoy the easy current.

After, we came to the first sign of human intervention, and in fact, it was a hand-painted plywood sign that read, "Private Property." Below, two arrows were painted: one read "San Marcos River," and the other "Dead End." In truth, the second arrow pointed up the Blanco River, which joins the San Marcos at this point with warmer and shallower water. Megan and I were tired from that last four miles of paddling, but we had determined early on that we would explore the Blanco, so we turned our kayaks up-current and began slowly moving forward.

It had been a hard trip through the twists and turns of the first four miles of the San Marcos, and we needed to stretch our legs and find some-place to fish without either being blown into brush by the steady wind or drawn downriver by the current. I knew that this short exploration might provide such an opportunity as the Blanco has become shallow in many places and dry in others.

About a half mile upriver, we came to a sand bar where I was able to stake out the kayaks. It was a good spot for wade fishing in two to three feet of water. We tied on a couple of chartreuse and white Clouser minnows and began fishing opposite banks of the river from the vantage point of the large flats we were wading on. Megan got a few bites but no hookups, and I caught and released a small sunfish, and that is when I heard the splash.

Just behind me, something made a sound like it had either fallen from the riverbank onto the water or had engulfed something that had made the fatal mistake of doing so. For a moment, I thought it might be an alligator as I had instant flashbacks to my youth along the edges of the Everglades. I pushed that thought out of my mind as I was relatively sure of there not being any gators in the Blanco.

I cast toward the spot where the river had just erupted a moment prior. My fly landed, and with my first jerking strip, I saw a flash of fish-belly and felt my rod double over like Poseidon had taken hold! Flashbacks of gators were replaced by those of bonefish as whatever I had hooked raced directly toward me and then turned and ran toward deeper water. Seconds later, a Guadalupe bass jumped clear into the air, its beautiful emerald-colored back shining in the sunlight. Two more leaps and a few runs later, I held him in my hands, unhooked him, and watched as he swam in an almost leisurely, smug manner back to the same hidey-hole where I had found him.

Sometimes it is best to exit the stage on a high note. After hooking that amazingly beautiful bass and watching him return home, we loaded up our kayaks and began our return to the San Marcos. As I paddled away from the shallow, hot, almost tepid waters of the Blanco toward the cooler depth of the San Marcos, several large garfish slashed at minnows at my bow. They seemed more at home in this warm, half-dried upriver, but I wondered about the fate of my friend the bass. How would he fare as the private homes and ranches that line the Blanco drain it of its water more and more each day?

Sometimes . . . oftentimes, I feel sorry for fish. I think about what it must be like for them in a world that is so adversely influenced by a species of overzealous apes such as us. I think about what they must be feeling during the summer droughts when their homelands dwindle and recede, and that they must sometimes survive in tepid pools where they gasp for oxygen and dream of raindrops. How would we feel, I wonder, if the situation were reversed?

I imagine a world where an aquatic species felt the need to siphon off huge amounts of our atmosphere so that they could drink it, bathe in it, and aerate their kelp gardens, and when they were done with it, they would flush it back up into the sky carrying all of their waste products, some suspended in the air and others strewn across the landscape. I wonder how we would feel if we had to watch the sky falling closer to the Earth each day and the air growing evermore tepid, harder to breathe, rarified.

When we reached the San Marcos and turned downriver, we came to our next big challenge, a dam some twenty feet high that had a dangerous overflow along the left bank. We had been told that we would either need to portage our kayaks around the right side of the dam or lower them with a rope over the edge. By this time, we were both exhausted from roughly five miles of tough kayaking through rapids and around obstacles. There was no shade here, and the sun was high in the midday sky, baking us in the Texas heat.

Pulling the kayaks over to the small cove on the right side of the dam, we caught our breath as I surveyed the possibilities. Sadly, portage was out of the question. What once was a twisting trail was now choked in poison ivy and too narrow in any event to get the boats around the trees and down to the riverbank below. My only choice was to send Megan down, carefully, along the trail so as not to touch any of the poisonous vegetation while I lowered the heavy kayaks by rope.

For whatever reason, perhaps heat and exhaustion, the kayaks felt like they were loaded with bricks. I had to pick them up over the four-foot-high wall on the upriver side of the dam and then lower them over the edge with the rope I had brought with me for just such an occasion; they were just too heavy to control, and the rope burned cuts through my hands as the kayaks one by one conspired with gravity.

At last, I made my way down to the lower river, and we drank our last bottle of water as we listened to the roar of the cascading river over the dam. As she put the water bottle to her lips, I heard Megan make an "ummmm" sound, and I immediately thought how wonderful the water must taste. Then she yelled out, "It's like lava!" We both had a good laugh as we drank the hottest water I have ever had that didn't have a tea bag suspended in it. We had another three miles to go, and our arms were spent. Down the river we went.

The San Marcos, like each Hill Country river, has many moods. At its onset, it runs deep and clear, then deep and lazy, hazy-green, and then deep and black, and finally, it runs shallow, clear, and steady, the current urging us forward but in a gentle manner. Just as it became its most lovely and we drifted beneath the arms of ancient cypress trees, we came to the place where humanity invades the river once again.

The river narrowed, and the water became clear and shallow. Soon, after paddling under a small bridge and over a short rapid, we began to see and hear the interloping of other humans. College kids and a highly tattooed, pony-tailed, middle-aged man all drifted together in their inner tubes, some carrying half-drunk pretty girls, others holding frat boys, another yielding a gentleman who had the look of a prison escapee. Each rubber flotilla had a tube that floated a boom box or cooler filled with beer. I knew that these beer cans were most likely destined to be tossed into the heart of this lovely spring-fed artery.

Don't get me wrong, everyone was friendly as we paddled by them; after all, this is Texas. Still, I wish that they understood that this place is more than cool water on a hot day. I wish that they learned as children that this place is sacred, and like all sacred places, it must be respected. If there are things missing in these brave new American times, the ones that concern me the most include the following: respect, awareness, empathy, compassion, kindness, responsibility, and courage. Nature can teach all these lessons, but first, we must have eyes to see and ears to hear with. We must want to learn. Nobody ever learned anything that they did not want to learn.

As we paddled by the drifting people who went to the river yet never saw it, I began thinking about how this river holds within it some of the rarest life forms on Earth. Texas wild rice (*Zizania texana*), an endangered species of grass, is endemic only to the first two miles of this river and nowhere else in the world. It is threatened by the loss and degradation of its habitat. The widemouth blindcat, a species of catfish, is the only representative of the genus known in the world and is found only here in a few underground caves. The San Marcos gambusia is an endangered species found only in the San Marcos River Springs. This lovely little fish has not been seen since 1983, so it may be extinct. The fountain darter (*Etheostoma fonticola*) is a small, threatened freshwater fish found in the headwaters of only two rivers in Texas: the Comal River and the San Marcos River. The National Fish Hatchery and Technology Center in San Marcos keeps a reserve population of 500 adults, just in case an act of man or nature exterminates the last of the wild population. The Texas blind salamander (*Eurycea rathbuni*) and San Marcos salamander (*E. nana*) are rare, cave-dwelling amphibians native only to the spring caves that feed the San Marcos River. Their blood-red external gills allow them to breathe deep within their underwater caves as they feed on whatever may flow into their submerged subterranean homes, including the endemic blind shrimp. I think of these creatures as I drift downstream passing the beer-swilling kids and Tejano-blasting city dwellers, and I feel sad for the river as I float by a submerged beer can.

The San Marcos tells its own story, and in doing so, it tells our story as well. Just as in our own lives, each turn and run defines us, so it is for the river. We cannot be who we are without a nod toward our entire journey. We are defined not only by the darkness and light, the depths and shallows, the times of urgency and calm, but also by how we choose to react to each turn, riffle, and place where we might rest in some shaded pocket water of life. Like each of us, the river is a historical landscape. It is no longer the pristine spirit it once was before the first human touched it, so very long ago. It has endured dams and irrigation pipes, drunken college kids and thirsty cattle, and yet, it remains intact . . . lovely . . . still holding a hint of its wild youth.

None of us can ever be who we are unless we take each turn and each riffle in stride. It all defines us, not so much what happens to us but rather how we choose to view the journey and what we choose to learn. Life can be a fearful slog or an exciting adventure, it's all about perspective. I choose to live a life of learning and of living with as much passion, purpose, and poetry as I can muster. I choose to embrace uncertainty and just keep paddling. I, for one, choose adventure!

CHAPTER TEN

Llano

For instance, on the planet Earth, man had always assumed that
he was more intelligent than dolphins because he had achieved so
much—the wheel, New York, wars and so on—whilst all the dolphins
had ever done was muck about in the water having a good time. But
conversely, the dolphins had always believed that they were far more
intelligent than man—for precisely the same reasons.
~ DOUGLAS ADAMS, THE HITCHHIKER'S GUIDE TO THE GALAXY

WE HAD TRIED TO MEET THE WHITE BASS RUN AT THE BEND IN THE
Colorado. Casting until my arm demanded I stop, I discovered that it
doesn't matter how hard I fish if the fish aren't there yet. I had been
talking to Gene at Hill Country Outfitters about the Llano and with
a local guide whose name escapes me, and between the two of them,
I devised a plan to try again for white bass, this time where the Llano
meets the Colorado near Kingsland.

I make it a point to love every season in these hills. The summers
can be brutally hot, and I often feel sorry for the fish swimming in

ever-shrinking circles, but I still have wonderful days upon the river in the early morning shade. Autumn is lovely, the lost maples turning bronze, mixing with the yellows and rusty-colored leaves of pecans and sycamore. The rivers run cool and shallow and ever so clear, and I must hunt the fish in their secret places. Deer stand silent at the river's edge, watching . . . just watching me, and then accepting . . . just accepting me. They know that I, too, share the space in between before and after; like them, I am living now.

Autumn in these hills feels like a solitary heaven. In winter, the fishing grows slow to nonexistent during the coldest of days, unless you go where the trout live, stocked or wild along the tailwaters of the Guadalupe. And then again, even though the leaves are gone, and the fish are sullen in the deep cold pools, the river teaches me patience. Drifting nymphs along the limestone bottom bring the rare surprise of a half-hearted strike. There is something about frozen hands releasing a beautiful fish that makes the sun seem warmer, at least on the inside of me. Still, of all these times, if I must admit it, like secretly having a favorite friend, I love springtime the best.

Spring rains bring millions of flowers to these hills. They come in waves like storm troopers, first the blues and purples, then the reds and pinks, and at last the yellow and white flowers that tell you spring is passing . . . catch it while you can. In spring, the hummingbirds return; they know the arrival of the flowers too. Soon, the Mexican caracaras and the scissor-tailed flycatchers arrive soaring overhead. The axis deer are in velvet, and the javelinas run through arroyos with piglets following close behind. And there is one more rite of spring in these hills . . . the white bass run.

Our drive to Kingsland was a beautiful drive, surrounded by wildflowers, the sun slanting across the cedar trees. The prickly pears were just coming into bloom, and more importantly perhaps for us, the bluebonnets were covering every patch of untouched roadside. In Texas, bluebonnets mean that, more likely than not, the white bass are running. There is something special about the springtime light in these hills. The light seems to brighten the bluebonnets in a way that makes them even bluer.

I have always been in love with light. I have loved the sunrise and the sunset; they are the same light that is simply "living out" different moods. I have sat in a camp chair near the glowing embers of a cooling fire in Africa and in Peru looking up at the starlight above. I have always loved the way the light plays on the water of a Hill Country river; how it colors the autumn maple leaves, and perhaps most of all, how it takes on the nature of rainbows with the leaping of a wild trout. I have always been in love with light.

One night I had a dream that I was gazing into the night sky at my favorite constellation: Orion. Suddenly, all the stars that construct him exploded, and in that moment, the sky was truly black. I woke thinking about light, its nature . . . metaphorically. What do we do when there seems to be no light left in the sky? The answer came to me . . . we must invent it from within.

As the morning grew slightly older, we at last arrived at the river crossing near Kingsland. We strung up our rods and began the long walk across the floodplain. Buff-white earless lizards rocketed across the sandy open spaces between mesquite. The river ran quickly under the crossing bridge, spilling into a deep pool, and then twisting forward around a midstream island toward the Colorado.

At the water's edge, we met another fisherman. He was a kind, older Texan, older than me anyway. He was dressed in the finest of fishing gear with a broad-brimmed hat, sun gloves, and an expensive-looking rod. "If ur look'n fer Guadalupes, you need to head upstream," he said while pointing his rod in that direction. "There's some good holes up that way," he continued. I asked about the white bass, and he said he hadn't caught any yet even though it was late in the season. He said he "reckoned it was on account of the drought." I agreed with his assessment more to be respectful than out of any independent knowledge. His rod was still strung up, but he had the look of a man who was done. Not wanting to crowd him, I asked where he planned to fish and assured that we would respect his solitude. "Naw, I'm done," he said while pointing down toward the Colorado. "Ya'll go try some of them deep holes downstream, and good luck to ya!" He smiled, and I smiled back. We crossed the river and began casting, Megan to the north shore, and me to the south.

Texas is friendly. It's as much a part of who we are as deer hunting and high school football. Smiles linger on our lips like Cooper's barbeque and Shiner Bock beer, and I've got to say that in most of the Lone Star State, the kindness and food are better than the scenery. When we pass each other on a country road, we wave and perhaps even tip the brim of our hats. It's our Texas way of saying, "I see you, neighbor." I love that.

These hills are, in fact, an island in the sea of Texas. They float below the endless plains of the Llano Estacado and the rolling scrub brush of the coastal south. Like any island, the landscape has limits . . . it ends. For generations, this has been a historical landscape of many peoples, and its story is one of how they each touch the landscape and how it touched them.

Our first casts brought a few little long-eared and yellow-bellied sunfish to hand and not much else. Still, it was a stunningly beautiful morning, the kind that makes you glad to be alive. We crossed the river several times as we moved down closer and closer to the place where my beloved Llano loses herself in the waters of the Colorado and then slowly makes her way to the Gulf of Mexico. I knew that the water swirling around my old canvas hippers would soon be among the coastal salt-grass-suspending tailing redfish and bathing, marauding sea trout. We walked ever so carefully through some very snaky-looking brush, watching for coiled diamonds or a flash of white cotton. Bluebonnets bloomed along the riverbanks . . . there was hope.

I worked my way around a deep pool that had a fast-moving inlet and outlet at each side and began swinging my silver Clouser down and across. It only took a few casts to put a deep bow in my rod. I was on to something, and it wasn't a bass or sunfish. At times I thought my five-weight rod might snap and the throbbing pull of a fish kept taking line, then allowing me to retrieve it, and then taking it again. A splashing fighting streak of ivory told me that I had just hooked into my first white bass.

Megan cheered me on from the upstream shoreline, and after a battle that seemed too long for his good health, I finally brought this beautiful, powerful fish to net. There was no time to dally; handling him with happy, wet hands, I unhooked him and slid him back into the pool where we first found each other. I was happy. Megan and I shared a hug. It was almost a perfect day.

As we continued downstream, I found myself feeling a mixture of joy and regret. I was happy to have connected to my first white bass and to have shared that moment with Megan, but I also wished it had been her who caught it instead of me. I guess any father would feel the same. For her part, she was just happy for me. For a moment, I stopped fishing and instead simply enjoyed watching her make one graceful cast after another.

We brought only one water bottle on this trip, having planned to fish through the morning and then drive to Llano for some barbeque at Cooper's. As the sun rose overhead and hunger began to pull on us, we began walking up the north shoreline across the sandy floodplains between the scattered mesquite trees, picking up the occasional brightly colored stone. I noticed a short trail cutting through a patch of brush and just on impulse said, "Why don't we see where that goes, and if it looks good, you can take a few last casts?"

At the bottom of the trail, we found a deep pool that had a large granite boulder extending into it on the downstream side. Megan cast her Clouser into the pool, and after a few casts to all the "right" places, nothing happened. I was standing on the bank watching and said, "One more cast . . . over there," while pointing to the only place she hadn't tried, upstream, breaking all the rules of streamer-craft. She cast and then, after letting the fly sink and drift, began her retrieve, and in an instant, her rod doubled over, and I heard her yell, "Wow!"

The fight was nothing less than epic, and as it turned out, her first white bass was twice as big as mine, and as she landed the silver-ivory fish, we both smiled in broad, happy Texas smiles, and we laughed and hugged when it swam away. Now, I thought . . . now, this was the perfect day! Then again, there was still the barbeque to be enjoyed.

On another trip to the Llano, I pushed the kayak forward into the flow of the river and paddled downstream across a shallow stretch of rapids and into the first pool. My fly-rod was next to me nestled between my right leg and the hull of the boat, most of it pointing back toward the crossing where I had launched.

Whereas I had established a rhythm of fishing every few days of each week, hostile weather and family obligations had conspired to deprive me of the river for two weeks. I could feel an edge growing inside me, a dark place that needed light. The tension, depression, anxiety, PTSD, whatever label I might choose to give to this destructive lack of equilibrium, soon began drifting downstream with my kayak. I was at peace. Nature heals.

In her wonderful book entitled *The Nature Fix: Why Nature Makes Us Happier, Healthier, and More Creative,* Florence Williams explores how being in nature improves our physical, cognitive, and emotional health. She concludes that "People are happiest when they are well enmeshed in community and friendships, have their basic survival needs met, and keep their minds stimulated and engaged, often in the service of some sort of cause larger than themselves." I have found that, personally and professionally, nature therapy can be lifesaving.

Standing in these rivers casting my line, hiking these canyons, casting away my cares, has helped me to become a more calm, resilient, and joyful person. We need wild spaces. We need the rhythms of nature. Nature saves us. Can we save nature from us? I pondered this question as I paddled down the river.

This is my favorite section of the Llano River. It runs clear and alive, both narrow and wide, across the limestone Llano Uplift. I have often enjoyed wade fishing the shallow upstream beat of this crossing but could never reach the downstream section due to the deep pools at the bridge and the thick, snaky-looking brush along the riverbank. This time, because I had a kayak, I was able to explore new parts of the river.

The red-winged blackbirds were singing on the tops of the mesquite trees that lined the riverbank, and in other areas where the pecan trees grew, cardinals sang their song. I only see and hear redwings along the Llano. The rivers of the Edwards Plateau seem to favor cardinals and wrens. A Texas rat snake was crossing the road where I launched the kayak. I stood there and protected him from anyone driving by until he was safely across. Baby map turtles lined each half-submerged branch; their parents swam just below. There is no need for glass-bottom boats in these hills; the rivers seem to be made of the molten residue of lightning-struck sand.

Guadalupe bass, yellow-bellied sunfish, gar, and carp swam beneath me, and a huge softshell turtle swam just in front of my kayak's bow. I watched as his long-nosed, beady-eyed face looked back at me and then disappeared beneath the water's surface. I paddled through each small rapid and then beached my vessel upon the rock islands in the middle of the river.

When I stop to fish any part of a river, I take time to just breathe and see and connect to that place. I take time to notice the sound of the water as it runs over rock and rivulet. I hear birdsong and the *plunk, plunk, plunk* sound of turtles dropping from their favorite sunning place. I walk with bent-over stealth around boulders and the river's edge looking for the spaces where the bass and sunfish are living. That yard-long run of water that is, for them, the whole river. And, after I have taken the time to "see" the river and the shadows reveal themselves as fish, then and only then do I select a fly and cast.

As I settled into the rhythm of the river moving each end of my paddle in small circles, drifting down current, over shallow riffles where the bottom of the kayak scraped on pebbles and rocks and then out to the first deep pool, I set my sights on a large rock island that lay, just ahead, where the Llano grew wide. If you do not consider the fish, birds, deer, frogs, turtles, snakes, lizards, and damselflies . . . I had the river all to myself.

Just ahead, my destination loomed, and the river split in two, running in a shallow riffle on the right and narrow, deeper rapids to the left. I spotted a channel that entered the rock island for a short distance and aimed the bow of the craft into it, running it up upon the rocks and then beaching it in the narrows.

Once on the island, I began scouting the surrounding pools and bits of pocket water. As careful as I was trying to be, I still managed to spook a ten-inch Guadalupe that was hiding in a shallow cove. I decided to start with a deep pool that was on the upstream side of the rock island just before the first set of small rapids. I tied on a fly—it is a local fly, simple in nature, consisting of a marabou tail and Estaz body. I tie them in sizes 6 through 10 on a streamer hook with the barb smashed down. I have no idea what they are called, but I call them "sparkle buggers," and they are deadly on Guadalupe bass and sunfish.

With my first cast, I saw the flash of a fish coming from beneath a boulder, and the rod jerked downward. It was a slashing strike that had me thinking "bass" until I recognized the throbbing fight of a large yellow-bellied sunfish. I worked him out of the current and brought him up, admired the yoke-yellow color of him, and went for the forceps as I could see that he had swallowed the fly.

I make it a point to always wet my hand before handling any fish, I crush the barbs on my hooks, and return each fish to the stream as quickly as possible. Still, I knew right away that this lovely fish was fighting his last fight. The fly was all the way down his gullet, and there was no way to remove it. Even though I quickly cut the tippet in hope he could survive, I saw the blood coming from his gills as I returned him to the stream. He floated away with a sideways flutter . . . this was not how I wanted my first cast to end. I felt bad. I apologized as he floated away. Then I told myself, "Who knows, he's a tough guy, he might make it." As I said it, I knew it wasn't true.

Nature reminds us always about the essence of life and death, how the former comes against all odds and the latter comes quickly and with certainty. That's how it goes; you do or don't get on a plane, and it does or doesn't crash. As a Marine and as a police officer, I knew all too well how fleeting life is and that we must grab every moment. This ever-present knowledge of mortality, in part, brought me to the Llano.

I never leave my family without saying, "I love you." I guess that's what happens once you've seen the light leave someone's eyes . . . once you've seen life go, like it does, like melting snow. It never asks for your permission, death does as it wishes to do, and it is always ultimately a solitary affair. It seems so arbitrary. Camus was right. Absurdity strikes when you least expect.

I've killed before, many times, on purpose. I have always been at peace whenever I lined up the crosshairs on a deer or a kudu and squeezed the trigger. Still, there is something decent within us that can always feel the "going." Nature reminds me about the gift of living. It reminds me that life goes on with or without us; this is the nature of things. Like Rick Blaine said in *Casablanca*, "One in, one out." The lesson learned is that life is lived in moments. Life isn't a dress rehearsal. We don't get a "redo." I gathered my line and cast again.

I began working the various coves and runs that tumble through and around the rock island and was catching fish on about every fourth or fifth cast, mostly Guadalupe bass in the ten- to twelve-inch range with a few yellow-bellied sunfish mixed in here and there. I also caught one fingerling-sized bass, bright emerald-green with no markings yet. After playing out the water around the first island, I relaunched my kayak and paddled through the next set of shallow rapids, island hopping and picking up a few more bass with each stop.

At one point, I was working a streamer in a down-and-across pattern through a deep pool that was just above the rapids. I noticed a large limestone boulder that was fully submerged at the far end of the pool, with a shadowy undercut beneath it. I cast just upstream and across from the shadow, letting the Clouser sink and then stripping it across the undercut, and that's when the undercut moved! My line tugged hard, and my rod bent deep as I quickly raised the rod-tip to set the hook and then everything came free, and the two-foot-long shadow moved back under the boulder . . . never to return.

I'm still not sure what it was. It looked like a moray eel or perhaps a land shark or some form of aquatic monster. I just stared at the place where the river bottom came to life, made a few half-hearted casts toward it, and then walked away shaking my head. After my encounter with the creature from the deep, it seemed like a good time to begin paddling back toward the crossing, hoping that the thing below me didn't have a taste for kayaks or middle-aged Texans.

The lazy trip downriver became an upriver workout. At times there was the need to portage along the edge of shallow rapids, and at times I just paddled through them feeling a healthy pump in my arms. Fly-fishing and kayaking give you that kind of sweet exhaustion at the end of the day that is a mixture of healthy exercise and inner peace. In part of the river, I could drift along, casting at leisure, not really trying to catch anything. I revisited one island, casting into my new favorite hole and listening to the rare sound of a bobwhite quail in the distance.

When I was young, I used to camp out under the stars to the sound of crickets and frogs, and I'd wake to the sound of bobwhite quail. Now, the little bird that I always thought would be here is rare in these parts. It's a damn shame. Among other things, their love of ants and the arrival of fire ants seem to have spelled doom to them and the Texas horned lizard. Sometimes humanity seems like a curse upon the landscape. We transport creatures from one place to another without any understanding of the consequences of our actions, and each time we do, it is like a bullet shot from the barrel of a gun; you can't bring it back.

I think what these hills, rivers, rocks, and even bird songs teach me is that I don't matter very much . . . not really. All that comes from my life is what acts of kindness and courage I can muster in the face of adversity, that is all. I am deeply connected to these hills and rivers. This place and I contain a oneness. We do not own each other; we belong to each other.

It's hard for me to really choose a single homewater. While the Guadalupe slides closest to my house, the Llano runs tightly around my heart. I guess I'm a polygamist of sorts. I'm in love with two lovely spirits, and when I'm with one, I give her all my attention but do not love the other any less.

I have a tradition when I fish the Llano near Castell. Of course, I must pay my respects at the Castell General Store to Randy, the owner, who describes himself as "the local color." On the sign in front, it reads, "Castell Texas: Land of the Big Cock." There is a massive stuffed rooster just inside the front door. I'll let Randy explain it to you when you get there.

It's a good place to get a burger and a beer and to hang out on the porch on a hot Texas summer day eating watermelon slices. The fishing is good anywhere along the Llano, west toward the headwaters and east past the town of Llano and on toward Kingsland. When I fish the middle areas of the Llano, I have a favorite tradition where I fish all morning then drive southwest to one of my favorite Hill Country towns: Mason.

The small towns of the Texas Hill Country each have their own personality and individual charms. When you drive across this landscape, the hills roll up and down, sometimes rising steeply and forming deep canyons and oftentimes rolling in a laid-back Texan manner where the first sign of upcoming humanity is a water tower, then a church steeple, and finally the top of the county courthouse. In fact, some "towns," such as Art, Bend, Vanderpool, and Vance, consist of a single church, a single graveyard, and a US Post Office that is most often closed.

Mason is a great town in which to be hungry. After a morning of fly-fishing on the Llano, I like to go to Señora Santo's Taqueria and sit in my favorite chair watching the small-town world go by. I know that if I want my favorite chair—the one in the corner where the morning sunlight filters through the garden and slants across the table—I must arrive early. This works best on those hot summer days where fishing through the midday is just too brutal, no matter how many times you dunk yourself in the river. As I write this, I can almost smell the fresh tortillas and see Señora Santo's smile when I walk in the door. She reminds me of my grandmother, and the smells and tastes here help me to recall the ones I knew then, before her passing.

As I sit in my favorite chair waiting for my food and sangria to arrive, I watch the people around me, laughing, talking, and just living. I think of all those who, through time, have had some quiet corner that they longed for, some favorite chair in which to sit, looking out upon these Texas hills. In these times, chairs seem to be invisible. They often sit alone and forgotten in a corner. People pass them by and move them out of the way, like the inconvenient homeless person who sleeps on a bench, which is itself just a big chair. They pull them up and sit on them as if they aren't there, or as if they are always there and, therefore, worthy of being forgotten. Sometimes, I have felt like a chair.

There was a time when chairs had meaning, beauty, and value. They still do, but the mass of humanity has lost the ability to appreciate their simple elegance. Vincent van Gogh painted a portrait of his bright yellow chair. The painting is entitled *Van Gogh's Chair*. It is one of my favorite paintings. He had only one chair, and so he understood its intrinsic value, like a man with a single lover.

There was a time when chairs were built by artisans. They began as sections of wood that began as sections of living trees. The chair maker never really made the chair, he simply released it from the wood, as they say ... whoever "they" are. That is the way of life and art; nothing is really created. When the artisan was finished, he could sit back on the chair and see what they had done together. He understood its meaning and its value, and like "God on the seventh day," he knew that it was good. We need to go back to the times ... when it was good.

Sometimes people are like chairs. They can seem invisible. We have become enslaved by our technology, slavery wrapped in the promise of freedom. These are distant and lonely times. We text each other in broken, dispassionate, semi-thoughts and walk past each other looking straight ahead. Like the chairs that we pull up without thought or appreciation we are now mass-produced, anonymous, and largely alone.

As I write these mental ramblings, I sit in "Steve's writing chair." It is a simple chair, dark mahogany in color, with a small khaki seat pad and an inviting nature. I love it and appreciate it. In the corner sits my "adventure chair." Made by hand in India, it is a dark, wooden camp chair with a seat, back, arms, and hassock all made of thick, dark, adventurous leather. From its seat, I have read many books of hunting in Africa and passages through distant lands. Both of my chairs are different. Both are appreciated for what they are and for the journey they have taken. I do not expect them to be the same or conform to my expectations. I take them just as they are. Maybe if we could find it within ourselves to stop to appreciate the handcrafted chair, with all its imperfections, we could then begin to accept the differences between each other. Maybe we could begin to reject the mass-produced items and plastic that surrounds us both in furniture and in the masses of people that used to be humanity. Maybe we should all take the time to sit for a while and think about that.

The late morning sun slants gently across my table. A lovely young Texas girl brings me my plate, two tacos with homemade habanero sauce, the tomatoes and lettuce always crisp and fresh. The sweetness of the homemade sangria cuts the bite of the peppers and leaves only the flavor. I am content in my chair. People come in, recognize me, smile, and say hello. There is a feeling of warmth in this place, a feeling lost in mass-produced America. Here, they see me, and I see them. Here, we share the best of human nature, and that, my friends, gives me hope.

I have discovered that mucking about in a river with my fly-rod and having a good time is the most intelligent thing I can ever do. I have lived to regret many of the obligations that were based upon other people's expectations, but I have never regretted a single moment casting my line into a river or listening to a canyon wren as he sang his sad, descending melody. It seems to me that bird brains and fish guts are wiser divining rods of how to spend our limited time than all the mythologies of humanity.

We are all mayflies who pretend to be constellations. In the big scheme of things, we don't have long to get it right, and we must align our own stars. So, I will leave the deadlines and multitasking to the idiots who care to waste their time flying toward the windshield of the universe. As for me, I will take the Llano in any season, and the Llano can take me.

CHAPTER ELEVEN

Blanco

*Men may dam it and say that they have made a lake, but it will still
be a river. It will keep its nature and bide its time, like a caged animal
alert for the slightest opening. In time, it will have its way; the dam,
like the ancient cliffs, will be carried away, piecemeal in the currents.*
                                                                 ~WENDELL BERRY

THE BLANCO IS A RIVER THAT FEELS AS I DO; WE COULD BE BLOOD
brothers. Born in the sky, we fell to the Earth and reemerged from
beneath limestone caves where we tumbled over rock and root toward
the sea, wild, free, living within the eternal circles of the universe. It is the
way of things. Over time, we have both let the artifacts of an uncivilized
civilization slowly, almost irrevocably, take away our freedom, separating
us from the universe.

Recently, I flew out of San Antonio International Airport, and as the
plane banked north toward Dallas, I could see the river below. I could
see the place where the Blanco meets the San Marcos, and I recalled the

images of the bass leaping at the end of my line in that place. He is still there, where a dying river joins a healthy one and, in this way, continues toward its destiny, at least for now. As we flew northward, I followed the Blanco with my eyes and felt saddened by what I saw. I saw stagnant pools of water in between long expanses of exposed bedrock. Like a long, curving stone snake, it still cuts through the Hill Country as it once did, except now the river hides beneath the rock, only rising here and there as humanity demands. The Blanco is damned.

The first time I looked upon the Blanco was at the crossing in Wimberley, Texas. I was on my way to a meeting for the work I did at the time, and so it was only a quick look at a lovely river that in that time was spilling across limestone and under massive old cypress trees. I couldn't wait to come back. When I did finally make it back to the Wimberley crossing, it was dry. Only the limestone remained, the same limestone that contains the tracks of dinosaurs.

The first time I came to the Blanco with fly-rod in hand turned out to be more of a reconnaissance trip. I drove along the river road east of the town of Blanco looking for a good place to fish. All along the road were crossings that were illegally fenced and posted. All along the riverbank were signs that read, "Private Property—No Parking." The river in these posted areas was lovely, often deep where the dams were placed with shallow, fishless stretches below each dam. I found an un-posted crossing where I could stand upon a dam and cast into a pool containing native largemouth bass, but I didn't do it. Instead, I watched as a blue heron hunted in the shallows and a banded water snake swam away from me and toward the hungry heron.

I decided that this would be a reconnaissance day unless I found a truly promising place to fish. I began to explore each crossing between the towns of Blanco and Wimberley. At each crossing, I found the roadsides were posted and the bridges also warned: "No Fishing—By Order of the County Commissioner's Court." The signs didn't read, "No Looking," so I stopped at each one, and I spent a wistful moment watching the crushed jade waters slipping away, carrying my hopes with them. I wonder if the Blanco and the San Saba are harbingers of the future. I believe that Richard Bach was correct when he said, "We are free to choose a new future." On that day, I never strung up my rod. On that day, I drove away feeling sad for the Blanco and deeply concerned for my homewater.

Winter came to the Hill Country before I returned to the Blanco. I read that Texas Parks and Wildlife had planted some stocker rainbow trout in the river within the boundaries of Blanco State Park. Even though I knew the native largemouth bass would be too cold to be active, I tried for the trout. Until now, I had avoided this state park. It is little more than a river access easement that runs through the town of Blanco and is visited by way too many humans for my solitary liking. Still, I found a section of the river where a wild and free tributary stream tumbled in and where there were no people . . . at least at first.

I was standing in the river casting into what appeared to be empty water when I noticed an attractive woman watching me from the riverbank. I said, "Good morning," and she replied in kind, only I said it with a Texan sound, and she said it with a heavy Russian accent. She said, "It is beautiful to watch you cast," and I replied, "My casting is often not beautiful . . . sometimes, I catch trees." She laughed at my honesty. She asked, "May I watch you for a while?" I told her that this would be fine, and so I went back to fishing for fish that were not there as Mila, my new friend from Belarus, sat in the grass beneath a massive old sycamore tree and watched me cast, sometimes with poetry, and sometimes without.

The river bottom of the Blanco is not the mix of uncovered limestone and pebbles that I am used to in the Hill Country. It is a mixture of fine gravel and slabs of limestone that are completely covered with algae and detritus from rotting leaves and other debris. The water is clean, but it is too slow in many areas due to the reduced flow and the many private dams. The largemouth bass can live in the deep, slow pools, but the Guadalupes seem to be all but gone.

I waded across the river, casting first along the near edges where the tributary spilled into the river and then out into deeper parts in the middle. The Blanco is wide in this spot, perhaps a hundred yards across.

Just upstream is a spillway where water tumbles over yet another dam. It sounds like a waterfall but is lacking the charm of natural falling water. My ears can hear the difference, like the difference between a musician playing sheet music and an artist improvising. Waterfalls in the wilderness are originals; spillways are poor copies. The river is a river, but here, it feels like a long, flat, shallow lake. There is almost no current, and this leaves me uneasy.

After a while, I settle into the rhythm of casting. I am throwing an olive woolly bugger down and across, but with no perceptible current, there is no swing to the thing. The river bottom was slippery, and several times, I almost lost my footing. Falling in the river would surely ruin any poetry that Mila might find as she watched me. I regained my balance and waved. She smiled and waved back. I worked my way up- and downriver, casting toward mats of floating aquatic vegetation and finding nothing but seemingly empty water. It's okay; I found solitude, and in this way, the fishing was good. I looked up, and she was gone.

Just because someone or something you love is under the weather doesn't mean you do not visit them. In part, the illness that leads to the river's damnation is the same as the other Hill Country rivers, only more so. The Blanco is drained by a million thirsty lips and tens of thousands of parched lawns, worthless in their alien greenness. Ranchers draw from its veins at the headwaters, but even more so, it is the homes of those who wanted to "live on the river" that create the most damage to the river. Like so many lost souls, they begin with the idea of, "Isn't this lovely?" and then, "Let's buy it," and finally, their human proclivity for rearranging furniture kicks in with, "If only it looked a little different." This is when they decide to build a dam across the Blanco.

There are many such private dams crossing the river because Texas law allows this. The result is often that above the dam the grandkids have a nice, deep pool to swim in, and below the dam, the river trickles above or below the bedrock. In time, it rises above the limestone once more and becomes a stream until meeting the next private dam, building behind its walls, then slowly draining beneath it once more. Like hatchling turtles running for the sea, each drop of the Blanco's water begins hopeful that perhaps, just perhaps, it will make it home. Is the Blanco a harbinger of the future of these once wild rivers? In time, will every Guadalupe bass become conditioned to be wary not for ospreys and eagles but rather for drunken college kids doing cannonballs? Nothing is irreversible. Nature can heal if we stop slashing her with our super-primate technology.

As I journeyed from river to river and canyon to canyon, the message became evermore clear; this story is not about me, really . . . it is about us. It is about salvation. This story reflects what we are becoming and how we need to stop, breathe, and realize that we are all running toward the cliff's edge and taking this landscape with us. Nature isn't just a metaphor for our true selves, it is a reflection. We should not look away. Wild rivers are the key to the landscape. They, like the atmosphere, give life. They carve canyons and carry our future into the circles that sustain us. Yet we treat our rivers and streams like slaves, to be used and forgotten. We treat our atmosphere in the same manner. If you think about it, they are one and the same.

Whenever I bring a fish to hand, I am aware that it cannot breathe. I can see it looking at me with eyes that say, "Put me back!" And almost always, I do. I use only barbless hooks and use my landing net sparingly. I try to keep the fish in the water as much as possible when I return him home. I treat him and the river with respect. Conversely, I recall a time when I slipped and fell into a deep pool of the Medina River. Foolishly, I had forgotten my safety belt, and my waders instantly began to fill with cold, rushing water. I had to fight to keep my head up, gasping for air, all the while thinking to myself, "Put me back!" Working my way to the water's edge, I caught my breath as I sat there listening to birdsong and thinking that if I had to die, this is a pretty place to do it. I also thought about how it's all connected, the water and the air. We need to stop rearranging the furniture.

According to the National Inventory of Dams, Texas has more dams than any other state, with over 7,500 legal dams that "block, divert, and slow waters of the Lone Star State." This number in no way reflects the many illegal dams that block, divert, and slow waters across Texas. The Texas Commission on Environmental Quality is responsible for regulating dam construction and removal. The enforcement of laws and regulations related to dam construction across Texas is almost non-existent. Texas has a strong "landowner rights" mentality when it comes to the use of water. This worked fine when a few settlers shared the land with a scattered few Native Americans.

The Texas Parks and Wildlife Department is supposed to regulate and protect our natural resources, and there are many things being done well in this regard. The introduction of nonnatives, including small-mouthed bass, has been a blunder that comes out of a working philosophy that the landscape is there to "serve us." Still, as much as they are trying to reverse this blunder by stocking rivers with thousands of fingerling native Guadalupe bass, they can't do anything to reverse the course on the destruction of our state fish's natural, clean, fast water habitat.

Each state's Parks and Wildlife Commissions must change their outdated outlook. Their primary mission should never be "providing recreation opportunities" for people, including anglers. Their primary mission needs to be protecting habitat and native flora and fauna. Their secondary mission needs to be educating the public about safe, sustainable, and respectful recreation. If they do this, all the rest will fall into place.

Texans must make this right. We must value our landscape as our heritage; anything less is a disgrace. We would not defile our Lone Star flag, why then do we defile our Lone Star landscapes? We must honor the Colorado as much as the Alamo. We don't own this land; we are a part of it, and it is a part of us. If the eyes of Texas are upon us, what they are seeing is not our better nature. We can learn to treat nature better. Texans must make this right.

Wade Davis wrote, "There are different ways of interpreting reality. How people conceive of themselves and their place on the Earth reveals much about their values." When he wrote this, he was comparing the worldview of the Hopi, Navajo, Havasupai, Zuni, and Paiute people who lived along the great river and the Euro-Mormon settlers who came not to live as part of the landscape but rather to conquer it. The Native Americans saw themselves as being connected spiritually to the landscape, it being a part of their being and, therefore, deserving the same respect due to any living creature. For them, the river, the rock, and the birds in the air were and are spiritual beings connected to the humans that live within nature's arms. For them, the canyon itself was alive, sacred, and holy. Land was loved, like family.

The White Mormon settlers saw the land as something that not only could be changed but should be changed into their own personal vision of paradise. For them, the landscape was a thing to be used. For them, the changes they made were justified by their God, and now we substitute government for God, so it amounts to the same self-fulfilling seal of approval. For them, land was owned . . . like a slave. If we think about it, and we should, this is the same mentality that allows people to build a dam across the Blanco River no matter the cost to the living water. Just as the Glen Canyon Dam destroyed a canyon ecosystem and submerged Anasazi cliff dwellings, the cumulative effects of the many little dams across Texas Hill Country rivers and streams ultimately destroy this rare landscape. We have no right to do so; we have an obligation to stop it.

It always strikes me as tragic how easily and irrevocably we harm those we love. All too often I see parents who say "I love you" to their children and then they cut long slashes through the child's spirit as they emotionally hammer them down into the image the parent has for the child rather than respecting the child's true self. All too often, people marry and say "I love you" and then they go about the business of trying to change each other. Perhaps many marriages end these days in part because we try to change each other. I think most people have no idea what love really is.

Love is the most powerful thing I know. It teaches us how to live for something greater than ourselves. It teaches us to take risk, to have faith, to step forward into the uncertain wind. Love makes us strong, even as we feel weakened by its loss, its memory, its shadow. When someone I love has left it unreturned, it may hurt, but it does not diminish me. When I look into the happy eyes of my daughter, and I hear her laughter, and I see her future, I know the power of love.

When we love someone, truly and without condition, we extend ourselves. It is the truest form of courage, and although it is a part of being alive, love lives longer than we do. I would not want to live a loveless life. Love is the most powerful thing I know. Love is when you say, "I see you," not for who you could be but who you are.

I love these rivers and streams. I love how they meander, and I have no desire to see them run straight. I have no affection or respect for canals. My fish don't need to be gold or have three tails. Fish do what they do, and that is fine with me. They hold in fast water, just behind a limestone boulder. They sip mayflies from the surface and minnows from the currents.

I love these hills, just as they are. I love how they rise and fall into canyons carved by the rivers. I love how they are covered with cedar, oak, sycamore, pecan, and mesquite. And I love how the deer and the wildflowers fill the meadows and how the long-horned cattle graze alongside the deer. I love these hills just as the glaciers left them; they cannot be improved with rooftops and highways.

I love our Hill Country culture, just as it is. We still wave and greet each other as we pass by and we say "Yes, ma'am" and "Yes, sir" and we open doors for ladies out of respect, not disrespect. We know that there is nothing wrong with hunting, football, or patriotism and that the smell of barbeque or the taste of Tex-Mex is as close as anyone comes to nirvana. In Texas, we are what America once was: honest, hardworking, and authentic. I love all these things, and I don't need them to change to fit my self-image or anyone else's. Still, we Texans must pay attention, or we will be responsible for the destruction of our own home. We can and must do better.

❧

After a while, I reeled in my line and began to peel off my waders. I did as I always did and spent some time just looking at the river . . . showing my respect for her. I still have hope for the Blanco. I still remember that day when Megan and I paddled our kayaks up the river from the point where it spills into the San Marcos. We found a shallow spot and posted the boats near a line of aquatic vegetation that was sending tiny white flowers out of the river and toward the sunshine. Multicolored dragonflies hovered everywhere, and birds sang along the water's edge.

On the way to that spot, massive garfish kept slashing at the surface just in front of the bow of our kayaks. I couldn't help but think of those four-foot-long freshwater barracudas when I stepped out of the boat. We each cast in different directions, and as always, I secretly hoped for her to catch the first and biggest fish. I was thinking that thought right about the same time my rod doubled over and I found myself attached to a hard-fighting, high-jumping bass. He was beautiful . . . like the river. He was wild and free and alive. That's how I felt, too, standing in that section of the river that still breathed water. When I set him free, I wished him well; the same wish I have for the Blanco. I wish the Blanco to be free.

Chapter Twelve

San Saba

I arise in the morning torn between a desire to improve the world and
a desire to enjoy the world. This makes it hard to plan the day.
　　　　　　　　　　　　　　　　　　　　~ E. B. White

One thing I've learned is that it is a good idea to leave certain
words out of my vocabulary. When I was growing up, I was told that the
word "can't" was not a part of my personal lexicon. This advice has served
me well and certainly paved the way for my career as a Marine.

One of my favorite authors, Richard Bach, once wrote, "Argue for
your limitations, and sure enough, they're yours." I believe this to be true,
and it has guided me in an almost pathological manner. In fact, many of
my greatest adventures, such as running a marathon, climbing a Peruvian
mountain, hunting in Africa, and even my time as a Marine, came about
in part because outside voices argued that their limitations extended to
me and I refused to listen.

Whenever I hear someone say, "Someday, I will . . ." or "I need to
. . ." I know that they never will. Whenever I hear those words coming

out of my own mouth, I immediately change them to action verbs as if writing a résumé or mission statement. I know that words matter. Stephen Covey used to say, "Everything is created twice, first in your mind, then in reality." I know this is true, so now I don't ever let myself say, "Someday I'd like to fly-fish the Amazon for peacock bass." Instead, I say, "I intend to fish the Amazon, and so I'm researching possible outfitters, rods, and ways to finance the trip." Action words lead to action thoughts and positive outcomes.

The San Saba was one of those "someday" places on the map. It was gnawing at me, just sitting up there at the top of the Hill Country like a mysterious little blue line, taunting me to drive up there and show it a thing or two. With my life taking a different track, I began turning a lot of "someday" things into "now" things. I restrung my guitar and began learning new songs. I finally bought that nice vise and began learning to tie flies. I began reading books for pleasure and as a means of self-directed learning or, perhaps more accurately, "literary adventure." I began taking better care of myself and telling the rat race to go to hell. And "someday" rivers began falling like dominoes. The San Saba intrigued me. I had never met anyone who had fished it, and I wanted to know why. So, I packed up my gear and began the long drive up through Fredericksburg and Mason toward Menard.

I did a little research before launching my expedition to the San Saba. The San Saba River flows along the northern boundary of the Edwards Plateau. It has two branches that run east through Schleicher County and merge near Fort McKavett to form the San Saba River. The San Saba once flowed for about 140 miles toward the northeast to then spill into the Colorado River. These days, sometimes it makes it, and sometimes it doesn't.

I learned of the history it holds and, sadly, how it may itself become history. With each passing year, the San Saba is disappearing beneath the limestone, and in time, only the dry-rock river bed may remain. Some of this is due to the years of drought and increasing temperatures that these hills and rivers have been experiencing. Still, the drought alone does not explain why the lovely San Saba is now one of the most endangered rivers in the United States. The San Saba is drying up.

There is so much that I love about Texas, but no place is perfect, and Texas has some antiquated laws, including those regarding the use of public waters. You see, each of these rivers is being drained by ranchers and developers who use the precious spring water to irrigate fields, water cattle, and sprinkle the occasional golf course that some profiteer puts in after he destroys a section of the Hill Country and places a sign at the entrance with the word "estates" within the misplaced name. Like the government is doing to our incomes, the San Saba is being sucked dry by all the eco-pirates who feel it's their right to take what they want and give nothing back. I had read of this condition and of how this river that once watered Comanche warhorses and herds of bison now often runs dry before reaching the Colorado.

Like all the Texas Hill Country, the San Saba is a historical land-scape that has felt the footprints of humanity for thousands of years. In 1732, the governor of Spanish Texas, Juan Antonio Bustillo y Ceballos, named it the Río de San Sabá de las Nueces. Ceballos was instrumen-tal in bringing settlers from the Canary Islands to establish a colony along the Rio San Antonio. Later, he helped establish the Santa Cruz de San Sabá Mission beneath the pecan-lined banks of the San Saba River in 1757 where the Spanish fought and were ultimately defeated by the Apache.

The Native Americans who camped along its banks included the Comanche, Lipan Apache, Cherokee, Waco, Caddo, and Kickapoo. It was along the San Saba that the Cherokees made their last stand before being defeated and captured by Colonel Edward Burleson, another sad chapter in the clash of cultures. Prior to the arrival of the Apache and Comanche, prehistoric humans lived here, leaving behind tools of stone to be found by modern-day archaeologists. I had to see it for myself. I had to stand in this river while it was still here to stand in . . . before, like life, it slips away forever.

I've learned that we all must be careful about slipping away. Lately, I've been concerned that I might slip all the way back into a pattern of "responsibility." Looking back, I have been responsible my whole life. Responsibility is overrated. You must be careful because it can sneak up on you and you can start believing in it too much like a new religion or some car salesman who says, "I'm going to go to work for you with my manager and see what I can do."

I've noticed that society puts a lot of lip service into getting other people to act in a manner that is good for society but not necessarily good for the individual. I bought into that for a long time . . . a lifetime, in fact. Most of my life, I have been in a responsible trance-like state, always at work early, working the hardest, trying to be everything to everyone who clamored for my attention to detail.

Sometimes, being responsible is like a disease, complete with its own doctors and recovery associations, as in, "Hi, I'm Steve, and I'm responsible." From time to time, I would wake up, look around me, and see that whole segments of my life had slipped away and that I was being used like a jackass pulling a cart full of nonsense up a hill. Sure, they may feed you at the end of the day but just enough for you to make another trip.

I had begun teaching, part-time, for two major universities, both jobs I found without looking for them. I just let them come to me. When I began this journey on the day my life changed forever, I came home and wrote down the following words: learning, teaching, writing, mentoring, and giving back. I knew whatever I did, I wanted to do those things.

When I teach, I do all these things. I've learned that the real difference we make in this world happens one person at a time. Sometimes, it is a sad truth that I find myself wandering around the halls of a university like Diogenes of Sinope, lamp in hand, calling out . . . "Does anyone care about student learning?" From the darkened halls comes the reply, "Have you completed the grant application?"

Still, each day, I do my best to be an island of free thought and exploration in a sea of bureaucratic hypocrisy and lemming-like political correctness. And I have been able to find a few kindred spirits who see the power and value of developing a new generation of open-minded, lifelong learners. You may ask, dear reader, "What does this have to do with fly-fishing and the meaning of life?" I raise my lamp and reply, "If the only hope we have to protect the places where we cast our lines is government, is there any hope?" The answer, of course, is no. Each action of value and every moment of kindness or courage comes from a single soul who chooses to care, and then groups of souls who choose to care and act together.

When I drive through the Texas Hill Country, with each bend and rise of the road, my mind clears, and for a while, life makes sense. There is something reassuring about the steeple of a church that rises above the cedar trees and speaks to the prayers of generations. When I pass through Mason driving around the courthouse square and on toward new countryside, my worries drop off me like autumn leaves in the wind. Ahead is a new river, and I will take it as it comes, and it will do the same for me in return.

The first time I had ever crossed the San Saba was in Menard, and the first thing I remember about Menard was all the gravestones everywhere. Each little Hill Country town has a small graveyard next to the local church. Graveyards, churches, water towers, and old limestone court-houses are ubiquitous here. They are like pecan trees along the Llano and cypress along the Guadalupe, somehow reassuring that the world still has some things that you can count on. Still, Menard seemed to have more than its share of headstones, and as I noticed that no one seemed to be in town during the day, it left me wondering what the nights were like. I whistled as I drove through town, visions of cabrito-craving zombies running through my head.

The river looked wide just west of the bridge due to the dam that crosses it at midtown. Just below the dam there is a pecan grove, and there the San Saba is only a few yards wide as it runs through wav-ing, green aquatic vegetation and over some rocks before disappearing around the reed-covered bend. I considered it, saw no fishable places, and decided to move on.

Just before reaching Menard, I drove down a long country road that rose and fell steeply through endless ranchland left natural so that your only indication that anyone lives there or "owns" it is an occasional metal gate. When I reached the river crossing that the guide book said held "good wade-fishing both up- and downstream," I found that the land-owners had fenced off both approaches to the shoreline and posted the increasingly common "No Trespassing" sign along each fence line.

The river itself was lovely, not the gin-clear waters I am used to in these hills but rather a semi-clear, crushed jade-green like I saw in the San Marcos. It would have been legal for me to just jump off the bridge into the river and wade it from there, but the bridge was about four feet above the waterline, and the pools on either side were at least four feet deep, and besides, I didn't want to risk being shot at by a rancher . . . legal or not. Instead, I chose to just sit there on the bridge and watch the river drift by for a while, like some cowboy version of Annie Dillard at Tinker Creek.

This place deserved this moment. I was sorry to find the fences and the signs, but I also understood, since people can ruin anything. If I were the caretaker of these gentle waters, perhaps I, too, would take care of them in this way. Perhaps I would simply place a sign made of rough natural wood, not metal, and it would read: "Please Respect This Living River." Education is preferable to legislation, whenever practical.

Beyond the edge of the bridge, the river seemed more like a stream flowing softly over massive rocks and edges of ancient limestone. The pecan and hackberry trees leaned over as if to hold the river and keep it from floating up. This was a silent place . . . a solitary place, where only the chickadees took note of my presence.

I regret that I could not stand in the rushing water, casting into history. It mattered, but not by much. I was already in love with the San Saba. She was like the lovely girl that you make eye contact with and you smile toward each other with that "if only" look, just before she walks away with the man she is unhappy with. I could tell as I looked into the river and down her soft, twisting turns that in another time we would have known love.

I thought of Annie Dillard sitting near Tinker Creek, watching it pass by, and how she wrote, "I've been thinking about seeing. I might see anything happen; I might see nothing but light and water. I walk home exhilarated or becalmed, but always changed, alive." This is how these Hill Country streams make me feel. I see them, like seeing a long-lost love from another life. And they teach me about being truly alive. They teach me about being authentic.

I sat there watching the light and the water and the movement of the pecan leaves in the morning breeze. I thought of Tinker Creek and of how living with simplicity provides clarity, like the flash of horizontal lightning in the evening sky or that moment when two souls breathe as one. Dillard was right when she wrote, "If you cultivate a healthy poverty and simplicity, so that finding a penny will literally make your day, then, since the world is in fact planted with pennies, you have with your poverty bought a life-time of days."

It is true, I thought, in this time my life has grown within my new-found poverty, and I am the happier for it. We must remember to notice the pennies. How many people drive over this lovely water, I wondered, and never notice how it shimmers in the sunlight?

Each crossing I found, from west of Menard to Mason, was posted and fenced. I spent the entire morning driving along the river looking for a place to fish. I refused to fish where the dam was in town. In town, it didn't feel like a river any more than a quarry could feel like a canyon. There were too many signs of humanity's handiwork: shaping, forming, controlling, changing, disrespecting, and taking from the river. They took its life in that space, even if it regained its dignity downstream at the spot in the road where I sat on the rancher's bridge.

I was getting hungry and needed something to take the regret away. Driving into Mason, I stopped at Señora Santo's Taqueria for some tacos and a glass of red wine. When I walked in, my favorite table was open, but I had decided to go next door and sit outside under the walnut tree on the sunny side of the Sandstone Cellars porch. I stopped by to say hello to Scott at the wine bar, and we talked about the hills, art, music, fishing, kayaking, life, friendship, laughter, and, of course, wine. Then I saw that Manny was outside as usual tending to the garden. They brought my tacos and habanero salsa, and as my head began to sweat under the sweet assault of the salsa, I sipped wine, listened to birdsong, and talked with Manny about the garden. Life was good. I couldn't even remember anything like regret. Instead, I was haunted by that lovely stream slipping through beneath the trees, just out of reach.

I told Scott that I was trying to fly-fish in the San Saba and of my morning of fences and warning signs. He said, "Did you try the swimming hole?" When you need to find your way around anywhere on Earth, ask the people who live in that landscape. After getting directions from my friend, I raised my glass and drank the last of the luscious red wine.

When I found the "swimming hole," it came complete with a small parking lot and a trash can provided by the county that apparently nobody used. There were empty beer cans, food wrappers, and the ubiquitous dirty disposable diapers strewn across the parking lot, around but not in the trash can, and even on the limestone that overlooked the river.

I don't know why but tossing dirty diapers into parking lots is a weird trait of a small segment of South Texas culture. In my estimation, it shows a decided lack of character. This is the only time I had witnessed such a disgrace in the Hill Country except each year when the pilgrimage happens at Garner State Park on the Frio. The same people who travel from Del Rio and San Antonio to the Frio each summer promptly denigrate the river with their trash, and until the park rangers clean it up, it begins to look like the slums of these cities.

It is important to note that no contractor ever bids to build a slum; people build slums. I thought of all the ranchers' fences and signs, and in that moment, I felt sympathy for them. After all, look at what happened in the only section of the river with public access. I decided that it didn't matter. It does, of course, but for that moment, I chose to walk down to the river and turn my back on the temporary scars left by humans who obviously have not evolved too many steps from the cave.

Once I reached the river, the world was beautiful again. It flowed over a shallow area that led to a deep pool, and for now, I had solitude on the San Saba. I stripped out my line and cast into the pool and got an immediate strike. My rod doubled over in that throbbing way it does with a yellow-bellied sunfish . . . this was a big one. I brought him to hand, a muscular, handsome sunfish that had that stunning egg-yolk yellow bursting from his belly. I slid him back into the San Saba and cast again.

It had grown very hot on this mid-summer day. Texas has two seasons: blazing summer heat and freezing winter cold. Sometimes we get both in the same day. I cast my Clouser minnow down and across the pool from one edge of the limestone shallows to the other. This place really requires a float-tube to be fished properly. Casting toward a rock outcropping, I got another strike, this time feisty but not heavy. A fingerling bass leaped into the air, shaking the fly that was almost as big as he was.

I love Guadalupe bass. They have so much attitude and are obviously Texans. When I took him off the hook, I said, "You're an overachiever, aren't you?" He looked back at me as if to say, "Shut up and put me back!" I did. I hoped he would grow up to be a big boy. "I'll be back," I said, in my best Austrian accent.

On the long drive home, I thought about the San Saba. I thought about her as if she were that pretty girl that you knew wasn't being treated right. I thought about how pretty she was now, and was once, and how sad it is to think that if things don't change, all this will be a memory. If I were a billionaire, I would buy it all just to protect it. But I am a part-time college professor and full-time wanderer who fishes in lovely streams that are connected to the universe. The only thing I have to offer these waters or these hills are my words. *Perhaps*, I thought, *my words can reach the hearts of someone who can save this singularly magical landscape before it's too late.*

<hr>

As autumn came, the hills finally received desperately needed rain. It rained for a week, and still we were in a drought. After the rains subsided, I decided to visit the San Saba again. This time, I drove to the town of San Saba to a new park I had read about that follows the river. When I arrived, I could see on the map at the parking lot that there was a trail that was about a mile long going to and following along the river. I strung up my rod and began walking through the lovely grove of pecan trees and through a meadow that was covered in autumn flowers.

It was still warm, and the leaves had not yet begun to change. I heard a familiar sound of a bird that is rarely seen here. I stopped and watched. Yes, robins had come, passing through on their way south. I continued down the path until reaching the river. I had read that, in these days, the San Saba is often dry here and that it doesn't even reach the Colorado anymore. This time, the river was a rushing torrent of muddy water. I knew when I saw the river that I would not be fishing today. No worries, I thought . . . it is flowing. There is hope.

As I sat next to the river, beneath the pecan trees listening to the sound of robins singing in the bent, golden grass, and watching that precious water drift by my feet, I wondered if the San Saba would disappear just as the Comanche Springs did on the year of my birth. Comanche Springs once flowed out of the ground, clear and cold from the Comanchean limestone near the town of Fort Stockton in central Pecos County. The springs gave birth to the headwaters of Comanche Creek, which was once full of fish and other wildlife.

During the 1800s, Comanche Springs was a Native American rest stop on the Comanche Trail to Mexico. The first recorded name I could find for the springs is *Awache*, a Comanche word meaning "wide water." Comanche Springs is said to have received its Anglo name when a Comanche warrior was killed there in a fight with white settlers who were using the springs. Later, it became the water source for the US Army Post, Camp Stockton, and, later, for the town of Fort Stockton.

Over time, the Edwards-Trinity Aquifer that was the spring's lifeblood was pumped dry, and by 1961, the springs ceased flowing. All the fish, turtles, frogs, and other wildlife died off, including the Comanche Springs pupfish, which disappeared with the water. Without water, there is no river. Without the river, there is no life.

The Texas Commission on Environmental Quality is ultimately responsible for the future of the San Saba. According to the national conservation group American Rivers, the San Saba is the third-most endangered river in the United States. With that said, it's important to remember that all the rivers in the Texas Hill Country are connected to the springs that give them life, and all the springs are connected to the aquifers. If the Hill Country is alive, and it is, what we are doing with ever-increasing velocity is hooking up thousands of intravenous tubes into the heart of the hills, and collectively, we are draining the life out of them. The "we" includes me every time I make coffee, take a shower, or wash clothes. The "we" I refer to also includes the Plateau Underground Water Conservation and Supply District in Schleicher County where the springs come from that create the San Saba. And then there is the

Menard County Underground Water District and all the ranchers and homeowners in Menard and Mason and Brady.

Ultimately, it is the economic success of Texas that is killing the Hill Country. As San Antonio and Austin continue to grow, demand for water increases. One short-term solution is for the Texas Commission on Environmental Quality to appoint a "water-master" to monitor stream flows and water use. As a Texan with a slight Libertarian streak, I'm concerned about government intrusion, and frankly, after working in government all my adult life, I have little faith in its abilities to "do the right thing." I understand why the people of the upper Hill Country are resisting this intrusion. Still, if no one is willing to come together and create sensible monitoring and management locally, then short of enforcement from Austin, the San Saba will die along with every fish, frog, turtle, and bit of wildlife that depends on it. If the San Saba dies, so will Menard. Who will tend the gravestones then?

In his classic story of the Colorado River and the Grand Canyon, Wade Davis tells of the human history of that great landscape and how human worldview makes all the difference in the eventual outcome. He writes, "There can surely be no greater crime against nature than to cause the death of a river, and no greater gesture of restitution than to facilitate its regeneration." I have nothing to offer these spring-fed streams, these wildlife and wildflower-covered hills, this rare landscape. I have nothing to offer this land that gives me life . . . nothing except these humble words and the hope and the passion for saving them.

CHAPTER THIRTEEN

Frio

You have to go to considerable trouble to live differently from the way the world wants you to live. The world doesn't want you to do a damn thing. If you wait till you got time to write a novel or time to write a story or time to read the hundred thousands of books you should have already read—if you wait for the time, you'll never do it. Cause there ain't no time; world don't want you to do that. World wants you to go to the zoo and eat cotton candy, preferably seven days a week.

~ HARRY CREWS

THE FIRST TIME I SAW THE FRIO WAS WHEN I CAME TO VISIT MY Marine brother Dave. I had been living in Montana and then in Florida after leaving the Marine Corps, and Dave had been trying to get me to come and spend some time with him in San Antonio. Unlike me, Dave was born and raised on the edge of the Texas Hill Country. When we were overseas dealing with Islamic terrorists, we had many long days and nights on posts waiting for the attack and talking of home. Defining my home back then was problematic. Today, I am clearly a Texan, but then I was a wanderer whose original home along the edge of the Loxahatchee River and Florida Everglades had been destroyed by unchecked overpopulation and development.

The last time I had been to the Frio was the last time I saw Dave alive. We had lived as young warriors through life and the threat of death and then time passed forward as it always does until it doesn't, and we found ourselves on the cliff overlooking the river speaking of these things: life and death. It was then that, for some reason, Dave decided to tell me his wishes if ever he were to leave this life before I did. Shortly thereafter, he was gone. His ashes were spread as he wished upon the Texas hills and across the landscape of the Lakota Sioux Nation, of which he was a part. Both places were a part of him, the Lakota grasslands where he participated in the Sun Dance, and the Texas Hill Country where I sat beside him during his pipe ceremony. In between then and now, I had fished this stretch of river only once. It was winter, and the water was colder than usual. I caught one tiny bass and one tiny yellow-bellied sunfish, but I was alone with the river, so the catching didn't matter as much as the fishing.

Now, a decade after my Marine brother's passing, I found myself driving westward toward the great Frio River. The Frio first trickles from headwater springs in Real County as the West Frio and from just above the town of Leakey as the East Frio. The waters slide over a limestone riverbed, sometimes narrow and sometimes wide, for about 200 miles until it joins the Nueces River. The water is pristine, clear, like liquid glass, and beneath it are some very large Guadalupe and largemouth bass that at times seem uncatchable.

Sometimes, fly-fishing the Frio reminds me of flats fishing for "bones" in the Caribbean. This can be true on other very clear Hill Country streams like the Llano, Medina, Pedernales, Nueces, and Upper Guadalupe. The Frio is perhaps the stream with the deepest clear holes and long expanses of freestone "flats" where Guadalupe and largemouth bass in the two-to-three-pound range sit motionless and perfectly camouflaged against the pebble bottom. Like bonefish on the sand flats, sometimes you see the shadow of the fish rather than the fish.

I had decided to make the journey to the section of the river that flows through Garner State Park and to hopefully do it in that moment

in time between when the water is too cold for the fish to bite actively
and when it's just warm enough for the "circus to come to town." I'm not
sure why, or even how, but every year as the water warms the Frio River
at Garner Park, it becomes the annual retreat for many families from San
Antonio to the Rio Bravo.

The people who flock there are not bad people, there are just too many
people, and as is often the case when large numbers of people migrate
to the wildlands, I am left wondering why they bother. They seem to see
nothing that is around them and seem to miss the point, simply bringing
the inner city with them, complete with basketballs and blasting music.
Prior to their descending upon the park like biblical locusts, this place is
silent save for birdsongs and coyote calls. When I arrived, I realized I had
come one day too late. The first waves of locusts were sleeping in tents,
park service cabins, and motor homes. I walked to the river and strung
up my rod in the last peaceful moments.

The Frio can only be described as lovely. It runs clear and cold over
rock and pebble bottom. It is surrounded by massive old bald cypress
trees where warblers call and squirrels scold as I cast below them. It is
alive with life: snakes, frogs, crawfish, turtles, deer, javelina, bobcats, ring-
tails, porcupine, and just about any other creature that lives in these hills.
Along its shore and within its belly lie massive boulders, and around the
boulders swim bass, sunfish, catfish, and the occasional garfish. For the
moment, I had the Frio to myself; after all, these are city folk, and they
sleep in while I rise before the sun.

Crossing at the park dam, I made my way along the far shoreline
toward the first set of rapids. It was early spring, and the flowers were
blooming along every stretch of the riverbank, even the aquatic plants
that reached above the water's surface displayed open flowers of white,
yellow, and pink. There are several deep plunge pools below the rapids
and then some deep glassy pools around the roots of cypress trees and
midstream rock formations. I could see the bass holding in the shallow
flats along the bank occasionally flashing emerald and silver as they
struck something just below the surface. They were feeding. In the deeper
pools, more bass hung suspended like objects placed in resin, and schools
of sunfish were swirling near tree roots and logjams. I tied on a Clouser.

The water was so clear that I couldn't see through it; instead, I saw the pebbled bottom reflecting into my eyes in many earth-toned shades so that a bass that was suspended directly in front of me is invisible, camouflaged within the kaleidoscope world. I found myself looking for shadows so that I could find the fish that were clearly in front of me, blending with the water and the river bottom.

A two-pound bass splashed away from my feet. Another perhaps larger bass cut through the shallows, torpedo-like, from near my half-submerged legs. I never saw them until they moved, even though the river is crystalline. I took a breath and refocused, not casting, just watching. I saw them now, suspended, watching me. I waded forward searching for my target, I could have been in the Bahamas, and there is no difference in the difficulty of this thing. And then I see him just below a half-submerged, Volkswagen-sized boulder, and I cast my fly that lands with a "plunk" into the clear, clear water, and he is gone. I waded forward.

Downriver, I could hear the circus waking. Tejano music was playing, and I could hear the intrusive *thump, thump, thump* of a distant basketball upon the park service-built court. I asked myself who the idiot was that decided the one thing a beautiful and pristine wilderness needed was a basketball court and dumpsters.

Across the river, I saw the movement of humans, not bad humans, just intrusive humans. A man and his children were casting bobbers into the pool I was moving toward, and the fish scattered. They spoke in the loud tones that people use when they come from the city and have a distrust of silence. I could hear in his voice that he was a good father; it held a kind and instructive tone. I thought of how nice it was that he was exposing his children to nature but wished they were exposing themselves somewhere else. I waded downriver away from humanity and toward the silence I trust.

In time, I turned the corner to a bend in the Frio where rapids ran, and I saw and heard only the river and the birds and the breeze. I cast long looping lines into the river, then let my streamer swing into the current and retrieved it. It had become more of an exercise in casting. I repeatedly spooked fish that I was sight-casting toward. Then I'd come to an area of aquatic vegetation over narrow running water.

The river was healthy, full of waving green plants and swimming tadpoles. Frogs exploded along the shoreline with each step I took, detonating like an amphibious minefield. I cast again, this time toward a swirl that was expanding along the weed bed; my line pulled taut, and the rod bent toward the swirling ripples as if divining the location of fish life. A jewel-like Guadalupe came to hand. Lucky shot. I released him.

Sometimes catching a nice fish causes me to cast again, not changing my recently successful fly, just keeping the rhythm of it all intact. And sometimes, the catching of a nice fish causes me to stop and drink it all in. I looked around me at the clear running water over stones and bases of old-growth trees that line the river. I saw the steady, focused flight of a kingfisher moving downriver, fleeing from me as I fled the other humans and their red-and-white bobbers. I took notice of the frogs and crickets looking for love, their rhythmic calls crisscrossing the water. I saw the deer drinking just down and across from me, and we looked and considered one another before she turned and walked away, unalarmed at my voyeurism.

As if suddenly coming into focus, as if out of a trance, I noticed the circular artwork of an orb spider overhead, strung out between the treetops. He fishes the air for mayflies. This was one of those times, a time to stop and breathe . . . to take notice of life. It was also time to turn around and begin working back upstream. I clipped off my clunky streamer and tied on an Adams. The water was just too clear to tolerate anything, but small flies presented as softly as possible.

I decided to move slowly upstream, casting as carefully as I could to the small pools near the bases of cypress trees, fishing leisurely without care of catching or doing anything in particular. I had noticed a few fish snapping at whatever was floating through the current. There were no mayflies that I could see, and the air had become warm, so I gambled that my Adams could imitate anything airborne or terrestrial.

The fish that were popping the surface were yellow-bellied sunfish, and as I knew that they are not especially picky eaters, I cast upstream and across with a slight mend toward the midstream current. The rhythm of it all became hypnotic . . . drift, drift, drift, take, again and again I caught one sunfish after another. Not caring how many or how big, and losing count at any rate, I just settled into it as I walked slowly upstream toward the pool where the bobbers no longer bobbed.

For a long time, it seemed as if I were the only soul on the Frio, and the sound of rushing water upstream masked anything that was throbbing above it. And then I reached the last set of rapids below the dam, and I could see the people swimming and hear the *thump, thump, thump,* of the ball on pavement and voices saying nothing, attached to eyes seeing nothing.

When I first arrived, I had noticed that just a short distance away from the campground full of city dwellers there was a field with a small herd of axis deer intermittently feeding and watching the early morning waking moments of the alien humans who were drawn to this place for its cool water on hot days, its pit toilets and picnic benches, but who had no real connection to the landscape. For them, this landscape was as incomprehensible as their chatter was to me. I noticed that the deer looked at them unalarmed, as if considering fish within a bowl. I decide that I am quite like the deer, looking in from some other world.

These were good people, mostly, enjoying a tradition with extended family that had been most likely going on for so long that they could not recall where it started or why. Pretty young girls chatted like chickens in their Tex-Mex language of Spanish and English. Grandmothers who reminded me of my own sat silently in folding chairs looking out at generations of playing progeny. While some young men played basketball, others walked in circles through the campground as if lost, as if wondering, what do you "do" out here? I found myself torn between the feeling of sadness in lost generations who saw no value in this landscape outside of the cooling water and of hope that perhaps one of them would, like me, find themselves in these hills and along this river. I believe if we are to save the Earth from us, we must find ways to help more of us learn to understand and love nature.

I snipped off my fly, broke down my rod, and took my lunch from the cooler. Walking along the river, I came to the same picnic bench where my wife and I first came here with Dave many years ago. We drove out from San Antonio in his giant, open-topped truck nicknamed "The Beast." He went to work right away setting up the grill and getting the mesquite wood burning. It was winter then, with a chill in the air, and the park was empty save for us, the deer, and some very large bass that had no interest in eating.

Alice and I walked up the hill to the overlook, and when we had returned, we found Dave fast asleep in a lounge chair, the coals white-hot in the grill. I woke him in the gentle manner we Marines have with each other, and after he caught his breath from the chest thump I gave him, we cooked up some sausages and borracho beans for our stream-side feast.

As I sat on the bench, my mind traveling back in time, surrounded then by serenity and laughter and friendship, surrounded now by the masses of transplanted city-dwellers, I smiled. I couldn't help but think that somewhere in this crowd another young man from the westside of San Antonio has quietly slipped away from the masses and is walking the lonely paths, not feeling lonely at all. Perhaps one of these young people actually "gets it," and for them, like me, the trees, birds, deer, and river are not invisible.

I noticed that my perception of this space had changed. Whereas the multitudes around me could not see the trees or hear the birds, in time, I found that the masses of humanity had vanished from my world, and I sat there on that bench alone with the river. The problem with enlightenment is that once you see something for what it really is, you can never unsee it.

Although I love to teach, my new part-time job as a college professor had given me glimpses of the imitation world that had rejected me and which I now reject. I have seen what lies beneath the magician's table and what flutters up his sleeve, and it holds no magic for me, evermore. Like a beagle pup escaping out the back door, I have been running free, and no amount of table scraps will lure me all the way back in. We sell our dreams, souls, and very lives while trying to "make a living." *Beware of table scrap offerings*, my inner voice warns. *Someone else is eating the meal.*

So I sat there, watching the river drift by me and a water snake swimming sleekly across the current. I thought of my brother Dave and how we would laugh together every time we were together and of his passing. I thought of a dream I had just after I lost my job, where Dave was listening to me describe my journey, a story he knew all too well. In the dream, he said, "Well, my brother, life is very short. Whatever it is you want to do with your life, you had better get on with it." I remembered waking up and feeling that the conversation was real and whispering in the dark, "I will Dave . . . I promise I will."

And then, as I watched an osprey soaring just above the treetops, I began to hear the words of Hafiz: "Don't veer off your own course, lifted by the wings and feathers of glory, because the arrow that flies high up stays there a moment and at last eats the earth." Words well written are like DNA . . . they outlive us.

When people act in a manner that emits their illusion of self-importance, it almost always makes me laugh. After all, like any warrior of the world or the streets, I know where the story ends, and in the end, we are all equal in our insignificance. It doesn't matter about our title or money, our power or prose; when the last page turns, "life" goes away. The arrow of my life is descending, but I'm getting some good hang time and am making sure I enjoy every moment. I still have a lot of living to do, and even if the earth met me now, what a ride it has been!

I've been learning a lot along the way. In my life, learning and living are the same. I learn a lot from hardship and human cruelty. It is important to learn the right lessons in this regard, so that when you pass the test you don't look at the top of the page and see "bitterness" written in red pen as your grade. So far, my grade reads, "understanding, acceptance, resilience, perspective, kindness, and courage." It is written in purple.

I'm happy with that grade, and I find each test changes my perspective a little more. I would trade wisdom for youth any day, but since that offer has not come along, I will have to have the wisdom to stay young inside. Life is about choices. I choose to be happy, to understand what I can and cannot control, to accept life as it comes, be resilient, and maintain a healthy, open perspective. I also choose to have the courage to put myself in harm's way and to stand up even if everyone else is sitting down. There is a price to pay for doing this, but it is the only path I could "live with."

There is a white wildflower that blooms in the Texas Hill Country briefly, once a year. It grows at the end of a long, green, tubular stem, usually out of the thinnest and stoniest soil. These lonely white flowers bloom like mayflies, only for a few days, and then they are gone. Still, in my mind's eye, they bloom each day, and this, too, is a lesson. Our lives are only as important or as memorable as our deeds. The difference we make comes in fleeting moments of kindness, courage, and silence.

Things have changed for me. Like any warrior returning home, I will never see the world in the same light ever again. I have been left bloodied by the battles of life. I have learned that sometimes, often-times, the bad guys win. Yes, I now know how each story ends, and I cannot reconcile my understanding with the illusion. I can't pretend anymore to believe in the plot and no longer want to play along and just say my lines like a "good citizen."

Harry Crews was right, "You have to go to considerable trouble to live differently from the way the world wants you to live." As I drove away from the river and from the circus, I reminded myself not to let the vortex take me down. Resistance is not futile, but it does take vigilance.

A red-tailed hawk crossed over the road as I crossed the river driving back toward Bandera. The Texas hills rolled out in front of me, and the evening sun reflected in the cedar trees. I thought of how many creatures live along the Frio, now and always. I thought of returning when the deer stand silent, watching a slightly past middle-aged Texan casting his cares into the wind. I smiled.

CHAPTER FOURTEEN

Echo Canyon

*You are led through your lifetime by the inner learning creature, the
playful spiritual being that is your real self. Don't turn away from
possible futures before you're certain you don't have anything to learn
from them. You're always free to change your mind and choose a different future, or a different past.*
~ RICHARD BACH, ILLUSIONS: THE ADVENTURES
OF A RELUCTANT MESSIAH

ECHO CANYON IS A DEEP, NARROW PASSAGE BETWEEN THE NORTH AND
south domes of Enchanted Rock. Sometimes at the bottom of the canyon
there is a stream, and sometimes there is not; it depends on how the stream
feels that day. Even when it's not there, it is there. Sometimes, the stream
decides to run beneath the granite rather than above it. There is nothing
wrong with this; the stream is teaching lessons of patience and impermanence and of how important it is to be resilient. I knew that I needed to
be reminded of these lessons as I had recently become disquieted inside,
thinking too much and forgetting to let go of expectations and just live.

It's true, you know. The perspective we choose is the perspective we live, or as Thich Nhat Hanh once wrote, "Sometimes your joy is the source of your smile, but sometimes your smile can be the source of your joy."

To reach Echo Canyon, I always take the long way around. You can hike directly from the parking lot at Enchanted Rock State Park partway up the rock face and then hang a left into the canyon coming in from the east. You can reach the canyon this way, but it is a foolish thing to do. Sometimes, and perhaps even often, people get so wrapped up in the destination that they forget that the journey is a part of the experience. I know this sounds like a greeting card saying, but it's true nonetheless.

Most people I encounter outdoors seem to be afraid of serenity and treat nature's landscape like Medusa's head . . . best not looked at directly. They walk ever forward with their heads facing down while talking loudly about nothing of importance. When I see this, two thoughts enter my mind . . . well, perhaps three. First, I wonder why they bother coming out into the wildlands so that they can ignore it. Then, I want to make them look up, see me, and, in a loud whisper, I want to admonish them to use their outside voice: "Be quiet." And last, I want to put as much time, space, and wilderness between them and me as humanly possible. Like Papa Hemingway, I can only love people a very few at a time. After all, I come here to be here, in the moment, within nature, wrapped in solitude. So instead of taking the path well-trodden, I choose my own path around the south dome of the great granite rock through the African-looking country and on toward Echo Lake.

The trail around the south dome, like all the trails around the rock, is covered in naturally crushed granite. I have always loved the way it sounds beneath my feet as I walk through the live oak, post oak, blackjack oak, and black hickory forest. Texas persimmon, agarita, white brush, and prickly pear rise between the boulders and the trees. In places, there are lovely African-like grasslands where mesquite grows here and there while mountain cedar clings to the higher elevations. Warblers and vireos sing above me, and spiny lizards dart between the grasses.

As much as I love the feel of the rock beneath my feet, the sound of the birds, and running rivulets of water that spill along creases in the stone, I may love the grasses of this landscape and the sound the wind makes when it bends them most of all. Waves of bent grass, buffalo grass, Indian grass, little bluestem, green sprangletop, love grass, and switchgrass move like envisioned music across the surrounding hills. I cannot walk these paths without reaching out to touch the grass as if my fingertips were the breeze. I see the ghosts of Tonkawa, Apache, and Comanche warriors reaching out as I do, in their time, in this place, which we each call home. And the grasses I touch are the same grasses they touched, transported through time by their DNA. Perhaps within that double helix travels our spirits as well.

In most of the Texas Hill Country limestone is the edge of the earth. Here at the pinnacle of the Llano uplift, the earth erupts as granite with streaks of quartz cutting through it like geological highways. This is the only place in the world where the blue-colored quartz llanite is found. The Enchanted Rock itself is a pink granite dome that rises 1,825 feet above sea level. It is one of the largest batholiths in the United States, but perhaps more importantly, it is enchanted. Paleo-Indian arrowheads have been found in the stream near the rock that dates back 12,000 years. The Tonkawa, Apache, and Comanche who lived here all believed that the rock contained spiritual powers. I agree with them.

There is something special about this place. It is an island within the island of the Texas hills. It is a unique and powerful landscape that rises out of these hills, which themselves are like no other. As I stand at the overlook on the southwest side of the rock, I can see the quarry just outside the park. A deep scar cuts into the granite, and blocks of its heart lay waiting to be hauled away. We killed the bison and removed the Comanche . . . will we not even let the rock be where it has been for 400 million years? I keep walking, head up, hand outstretched toward the waving grass.

Turning a corner in the path, I startled a white-tailed buck. He possessed thick main beams that boasted ten long, upturned points, each held high as he bounded over agarita and opuntia cacti. After climbing the next rise in the trail, I found myself standing at the water's edge, looking across Echo Lake. I have walked past this little lake many times always saying, "Someday, I'm going to bring my fly-rod with me," and today was that day. Echo Lake is more of what most people call a pond and we Texans call a tank. It really doesn't matter what we call it; names do not define it. Like wildflowers and dragonflies, it is just as lovely, even without a name.

Before making my first cast, I looked out across the water and remembered the time when my father taught me how to keep a promise. I remember this each time I look across wild, still water. We had been planning a fishing trip together for some time, and it seemed to me like an eternity. When you are seven years old, a month feels like forever, and a Hill Country lake seems like the farthest corners of the Earth. This was going to be my first real adventure. We were going to leave as the sun was setting, driving off into the starlight, into the realm of men.

A few days before the great day arrived, I found out that my grandfather had caught wind of the trip and had asked my father if he and my cousin Jerry could come along. I now know the pressure he must have felt to keep his promise to me without offending my grandfather. So, along he and Jerry came, and I sat not in the front seat with my dad but rather in the back seat with Jerry. It was okay since the drive wasn't part of the promise. I knew that we would still have our own boat, just Dad and me, and that we would still have the adventure. As I looked out into the unknown darkness and the silhouettes of trees disappeared into the blue-black moonlight, I knew that, somehow, he would keep his promise.

After a time, we arrived in the area of the big lake. We stopped at a diner, one of those sleek, silver-sided aluminum diners where they served up pancakes late at night and the waitresses laughed with your dad and embarrassed you by saying you were cute when all the while you were trying to be a man. The whole look, the smell, and the sounds of that diner . . . shining in the darkness . . . evoked the feel of adventure. It was all that I had hoped it would be. It was full of late-night travelers, fishermen, and hunters. And I was eating pancakes well past my bedtime. At last, I was a man on a man's trip. And then it began to rain, and as the rain came down, my cousin began to complain that the pancakes were not setting with him right, and he held his stomach and moaned.

The rain was falling faster now, and my grandfather suggested we turn back for home and that the trip was over. I looked at my dad, and he looked at me, and we got into the car and drove back in silence to take my grandfather and cousin home. When your dreams fall like rain through a dark, dark night, they make a sickening sound when they hit the ground. When they hit the ground, they sound like empty, like lonely, like betrayal. The rain just kept falling all the way home.

When we got home, we pulled into the garage so as not to be soaked by the rain. I would not have cared. Nothing is wetter than the disappointment you keep inside; nothing is colder than heartbroken. Mom greeted us and told Dad to come on in, and she would make some coffee to warm him up and hot chocolate for me to do the same. She took our pillows out of the old wood-sided station wagon we were planning to sleep in, and that is when it happened. My dad said, "What are you doing?" Everything stopped. Then he said, "I told my son that we are going fishing at the lake, and by God, we are going!" Dad took the pillows and put them back in the car. We took the hot coffee and cocoa to go, and as we drove through the darkness, I sat up front with a man, feeling like a man. A man keeps his promises.

The next morning, we woke after a night of hearing the rain pelting the side of the car. The stars were out, the sky had cleared, and as we went into the office of the lake lodge, I saw the great old tackle on the walls and the mounts of huge fish, and I can tell you with all certainty as someone who has now hunted the wilds of Africa . . . no greater adventure was ever had by any two men as we had in a johnboat that day of catching bluegill sunfish. I have never forgotten the lesson of that cold, rainy night; the lesson was about the value of a promise.

In these times, it seems to me that all of America has forgotten how to keep its word. Every day, people say to me, "We'll do lunch soon," or "I'll email you," or "Let's get together and catch up," and sometimes they even say "I love you," but nobody ever seems to see the value that those words should have or must have . . . if ever we have a chance of survival. Today in America, people don't have relationships, they have e-relationships. Our youth are losing the ability to talk and listen and have true friendships. Today, trust is gone, faith is gone, and now it seems too much trouble to even use a whole word . . . and OMG, there is nothing about that to LOL about.

And now, I am the father, and my daughter is my favorite fishing buddy. We spend real time, not virtual time, together on the river, with the trees and the fish and the birds and each other. Sometimes we talk, and sometimes we just are, and nothing needs to be said. And one thing is for sure and for certain, whenever she is visiting home and I tell her that we are going fishing together . . . nothing on heaven or Earth will keep me from keeping my promise. After all, my father taught me that by keeping a single promise, you can move a lifetime.

—✤—

I heard a splash at the water's edge and then another and another in quick secession, and the sound brought me back into the moment. I could see a very big largemouth bass swirling around like a shark, very excited about something. The brush on that side of the lake was too thick to get through, and the water was too deep to wade through. I just couldn't reach him.

Along another brushy edge, a smaller, perhaps one-pound bass leaped into the air, almost landing on the shore. It collided with a mesquite tree branch and fell back into Echo Lake. Soon the entire lake was alive with fish crashing into the surface, and it was then that I noticed that what they seemed to be hitting were the swarms of small, bright-blue dragon-flies that were dipping and diving across the surface.

These days, with the passing of time, like the rock, I've been wearing down. Tying on a fly can be a challenge because if I forget my glasses, as I had done this day, I can't see the tippet or the eyehook; it's all just a blur that doesn't get much better no matter how far I extend my arms. And even when I have my glasses, I find that my hands just don't work as well as they used to, and my fingers become clumsy as they lose control of the tag end or otherwise unravel the fledgling knot.

Sometimes it's disconcerting, and I wonder . . . will the one activity I love most also someday be taken from me? I have heard that after living past the half-century mark, life begins to take things back. Still, I'm like the granite dome of rock above me. I'm stubborn. I don't give in to wind, rain, sun, or fading eyesight that easy. In this case, despite all the evidence of what the fish were feeding on, I had already tied on an olive woolly bugger, and I knew I didn't have a dragonfly or damselfly pattern with me, so I went with it. After all, these are largemouth bass, not brook trout . . . right?

My casting was skillful that day. Tight loops rolled back just between the oak, cedar elm, and mesquite tree branches and then stretched out perfectly across the flat surface of the lake. Whenever this happens, and I have a "good casting day," I am amazed because I'm not that good. In fact, whenever I'm on a river and casting like Lefty Kreh's avatar, I know that I will have the place to myself. The only time anyone ever rounds a corner when I'm fishing is directly after I hang my line in a cypress tree or hook a submerged log.

When I hang up in a tree, they seem fascinated by the intricacies of my unraveling a knot that I couldn't consciously create if my life depended upon it. And whenever I inadvertently latch on to a submerged log or limestone ridge and someone is watching from the riverbank, they invariably say, "Hey, you hooked a big one!" Conversely, whenever I'm in the zone and everything is coming together, only the red-winged blackbirds and the white-tailed deer are there to see it, and they don't care. I've found that neither red-winged blackbirds or white-tailed deer impress easily.

I guess I fly-fish the same way I play guitar, and perhaps that is a shame. When I was twelve, my parents divorced, and thus an unhappy and lonely childhood became only lonely. My dad had problems of his own. He had lost his family, and he instantly became a single father to a twelve-year-old boy. I think he felt he lost a degree of his manhood as well. I understand this now that I'm older and have had life cut little pieces out of me. Before going out to reclaim his masculine spirit, he handed me a guitar and taught me three chords: G, C, and D. Then he said, "This will be your friend, always." He was right.

Somehow, I don't know how, I learned many new chords. I developed a real passion for playing blues, and soon, I was playing simple leads, mixing rhythm and lead as I felt I should, following no rules, since I didn't know any rules. Sometimes my dad would hear me play, and he'd ask, "How'd you learn that?" I'd tell the truth, "I don't know . . . I just did."

I guess if I'd take lessons, I could be good, or at least . . . better. I can't read music and have steadfastly refused to learn the technicalities of guitar playing. You see, for me, it's natural. I follow no rules. I just move as the mood leads me. Like a Hill Country stream, I just flow. Why would a stream ever want to become a canal?

For me, fly-fishing feels natural. The rivers teach me about my front cast, and the tree branches teach me about my backcast. The fish teach me about presentation, and the birds just sort of sit there in the trees watching. Whenever I read about how some guy uses so many beads of number whatever split-shot exactly whatever-many inches above his hand-tied leader that is made of whatever and whatever diameter hydro-whatever monofilament with a specialty-tied tungsten bead, lead-wrapped, two-handled golly-wonker nymph that must be cast at forty-five degrees to the coefficient of the current speed and average river depth . . . I turn the page.

I'm not a scientific angler and have no desire to mess up art and spirituality with facts. I learned to cast well enough to have a lifetime of enjoyment, and I catch fish almost every time I go out, so why screw up a good thing? I'm not saying that I'm not open to learning how to tie a new fly or improve my casting. The simple truth is, one of the things about fly-fishing that is most attractive to me is that you can do it for a lifetime and never stop learning. I'm just saying, I don't want something that I find to be fun, relaxing, and even spiritual to become work.

As I cast across Echo Lake in a methodical fashion, it became apparent that the bass thought they were brook trout, and they were having nothing of the streamer I was tossing, skillfully or not. They were eating dragonflies and had no use for my olive-colored bits of feather. Looking in my various fly boxes, I confirmed that I had, in fact, come out here without a single dragonfly or damselfly pattern. Note to self: Buy or learn to tie dragonflies. The closest thing I could find was a slightly bluish-tinged panfish popper. I tied it on and tossed it. I decided to pretend it was a dragonfly.

The real bugs were being hit as they dipped onto the water to deposit eggs. If they dallied too long, they were either picked off by some variety of sunfish or the water opened as they were engulfed by a largemouth bass. I'd cast it and let it sit for a moment, then recast it and repeat. On about my third try, I took a vicious strike that splashed water into the air but gave no indication as to the fish that delivered it. My Winston 5 weight doubled over, and for a second, I was hopeful of a largemouth bass, but then the bearing-down, fully submerged fighting style told me I had a big sunfish on the line. When it came to my hand, I found it was the largest bluegill I'd ever seen. I never catch bluegill when I'm fishing the fast-moving rivers and streams of the Hill Country, but here, in still water, they are at home. He filled my hand with his thick, colorful body as I slid him back into the lake to fight another day.

The sight of this little lake made me remember a childhood adventure where bluegill is all that I ever caught. The sight of my catch sliding back into the lake and swimming away pleased me but also brought a sense of melancholy. It is good that memories can live inside us. It is sad that they do not easily outlive us. Perhaps that is what words are for, giving memories and life lessons as gifts to whoever reads the hieroglyphics we scratch upon the parchment.

In time, it became apparent that although fish were striking dragonflies all around me, I couldn't buy another strike with anything I had in my fly box. I reeled in my line, and then I paused for a moment to just breathe, and be, and to just watch it all unfold around me: life and death. I watched as the sapphire-blue dragonflies dipped and landed upon the water and, in doing so, ensured another generation. I watched as the bluegill and the bass ate the hopeful parents one by one, thus ensuring their own survival for at least a little while longer. Nature isn't fair . . . it's honest.

Sometimes when I'm walking in silence, things can sneak up on me. Those demons that hunt us from within live in the silent, dark places, and if we let them, they remind us that no matter how far we travel, they are there, just beyond the moment, looking over our shoulder. Only the rushing, tumbling, plunging streams and rivers bring me peace.

Rivers and streams seem to carry me away, or more correctly, they carry away the detritus of life. Like a spring rain-shower, they wash me clean, and I am left standing there, waving a fulcrum, trying to be graceful, just me . . . whole again. Without the rivers to cleanse my spirit, I would have been crushed beneath the flotsam long ago. I owe my life to fast-moving rivers.

Walking from Echo Lake into the canyon is always magical. With my rod stored in my pack, I began the journey between the north and south domes of Enchanted Rock along the tiny creek and under the walnut, hickory, and cedar elm trees. The canyon is cool even if the sun is warm, and it holds a church-like quality of serenity, hopefulness, and eternity. The tiny stream trickles over the rocks, and wrens sing from the canyon walls. Tadpoles wiggle in the stream; they are always a sign of a healthy landscape. Looking up the canyon wall, I see a roadrunner hunting lizards. I scan the bushes . . . no coyote awaits him.

As I come to the narrowest portion of Echo Canyon, the trees give way to open sky, and each crack in the granite sprouts white flowers and thousands of bees. As with tadpoles, I'm always pleased to see bees. Still, there were just too many, and I'm never sure if what surrounds me are natives or Africanized invaders. I elect to climb the steep canyon wall to the top of Enchanted Rock.

With my pack securely upon my back and my cherished hiking stick in hand, I began climbing. Sometimes I could climb while standing upright, and in other places, I had to use handholds to pull myself up along the cracks and across the exfoliating, pink granite slabs. Occasionally, I'd stop to look back down into the narrow canyon or to listen to the canyon wren song while I caught my breath. A beautiful collared lizard darted just in front of me and then ran into a crevice in the granite. Once on top, I am in another world, the land of the granite rock community of plants and wildlife.

Most people who climb Enchanted Rock seem to miss the point of being there. They climb from the state park parking lot up the trail that goes directly to the top. Then, they look down toward where their car is parked and start back down to it so that they can get back into town in time for lunch. I avoid this place in those times. Instead, I come on the weekdays when I know that almost no one will be here. When I come here, I do so when it is only me, and the grass, and the birds, and the wind, and the enchanted, sacred stone. When I sit on top of this massive granite uplift, I don't look down . . . I look in.

Before climbing down from the dome of granite, I sat for a while as I always do and just took in the great expanse of the Hill Country. During these times, I try not to think. I try to just be present and notice how the wind bends the grass and the sun warms this enchanted stone. Still,

I did think about that past few months, years, and lifetimes. I thought about the great joys and sorrows of the past fifty years and about how I've overcome each challenge. Perhaps I have become just a little sadder for each lost illusion, or perhaps I have become just a little freer. I hope I am the latter.

I'd been spending almost all my time and effort on my part-time college teaching position, a work that I love, but a work that is also uncertain. It had been over a month since I'd last cast a line in a river, and the world had been creeping into my spirit and eroding my resolve. I thought of how recently the nagging outside voices have been whispering questions in my ear. What is coming next in my life? How will I make my living? Will I have a house to live in? What if this great experiment of authentic living fails?

Perhaps the rock spoke to me, or perhaps it was the wind or even something we call God, but some inner voice that sounded a lot like my own reminded me to tell those outside voices to go to hell. It was then that I remembered to let go and to cast my line into the wind with no end in mind. After all, it is about the fishing, not the catching. What will be will be. At that moment, I reaffirmed my determination not to turn away from possible futures before I'm certain that I don't have anything to learn from them. I reminded myself that I am always free to "change my mind and choose a different future or a different past." We all are free in this way.

In a sense, I did choose a different past. I chose to remember life's great lessons and turn them into a gift. It is in hardship that we are all defined. I choose to show off my scars, not hide them. Life isn't about being knocked down; it's about getting back up. In the past, I have gotten up and regained the fight head-on; this time is different. This time, I'm choosing a different future, the one I began with.

So, I'm not playing the game anymore. I'm going to cast my line in the direction of my choosing. I'm going to do what comes naturally. It's like playing the blues; I'm letting life's rhythm lead me . . . just flowing, sometimes above and sometimes below the rock, depending on how I feel. After all, why would a free-flowing stream like me ever want to risk becoming a canal?

CHAPTER FIFTEEN

San Gabriel

Not that I want to be a god or a hero. Just to change into a tree, grow for ages, not hurt anyone.

— CZESŁAW MIŁOSZ

WHEN I FIRST READ ERNEST HEMINGWAY'S NICK ADAMS STORIES, I liked them. I especially liked the story of Nick fly-fishing on the Big Two-Hearted River. I was a kid then, and the real meaning eluded me. When I returned home from my time in the Marine Corps, after the death of my best friend, and after the death of my happy illusions, I read it again. This time I understood everything, and I knew that I had been transformed, as were the rivers that reflected my now battle-scarred face.

Whenever I see my own reflection, I see what is behind the lines that radiate from weary eyes, behind any optimistic smile, and behind the scars. I am reminded of a favorite William Stafford poem: "They tell how it was, and how time came along, and how it happened again and again. They tell the slant life takes when it turns and slashes your face as a friend. Any wound is real. In church, a woman lets the sun find her cheek, and we see the lesson: there are years in that book; there are sorrows a choir can't reach when they sing. Rows of children lift their faces of promise, places where the scars will be."

All my adult life, I have searched for some balance between my existence as a warrior and the peace for which I yearn. I know that I am both warrior and poet inside, and although both spirits are true, I'd rather paint with words than pieces of lead. All my adult life, I have carried a firearm not only as an implement of the hunting ethic but as an implement of war.

As a Marine, I always had my M-16, Uzi, pistol, or shotgun by my side. They were extensions of my being, and they sent fast, hot lead toward any target that my mind willed them to impact. As a Texas Master Peace Officer, my pistol, shotgun, and AR-15 have served the same purpose. I have spent many hours training young warriors; in fact, I've made my living at it for many years.

I have lived my life striving to focus on what is beautiful and yet have always understood the evil that waits out there. Throughout this journey, my spirit has yearned for a time when I no longer live with the threat of conflict, deadly or otherwise. I have grown weary of humanity's darkness and wish to focus my eyes toward its distant flickering light. I have ached for the day when the only arm I ever raise is my casting arm.

One week before Christmas, I found out that one of the young peace officers that I had trained at the academy was shot in the head by armed robbers. He was a kid not too long ago. I remember his smile. When I first heard the news and that he was still alive, I suspected he was standing in a place where I have stood, at the river's edge, not knowing if he will make the crossing.

I wondered if he was peaceful. I wondered if he could feel his wife's hand in his. How many young men and women have lived this moment, in Iraq, in Afghanistan, in the streets of our cities? And then, just a few days ago, I learned that he had died. I felt that old, empty feeling that makes me hate the sound of bugles and formations of jets overhead. In the end, there is no end, and nothing is good or bad, it just is. Nature reminds me of this. The river teaches me to remember.

Through my years as a Marine and as a peace officer, I have crossed paths with many good souls who have worn the same uniform as I. Some are still here, and some have crossed over. As a former police chief and police academy director, I cringe every time I hear of another officer killed or wounded, and I wonder if they were ever one of "my troops" . . . not that this matters, except to me. I have always worried about them not because I doubt how good they are but because I know how evil the world can be.

I know how life unfolds as it does, like pieces of burning parchment. I know that our lifetime will come and go when we least expect it, no matter our theology. I know that this world is safer not because academicians and politicians debate the ethics of issues but because we few "rough men (and women) stand ready to do violence on their behalf."

Those of us who live this warrior life all chose or perhaps are chosen to live by the creed: "If not me, then who?" Ultimately, we know that our lives only matter in as much as we use them wisely to do some greater good. Still, lately, I have wondered if my time on the battlefield is ending. Maybe this is the vision I had of being alone on the battlefield, smoke blowing across my battered face, the broken grass bending in the breeze. I noticed that in that recurring vision I am sitting on a rock in much the same way I do when watching a river. Both on my visionary battlefield and my dreamscape rivers, I am waiting, watching, discerning . . . "What next?"

Fly-fishing seems to bring me to my senses perhaps even more than birdsong, or the gentle bending of grass, or how leaves drift to the earth, homeward. Inclement weather, family obligations, and my desire to give all I can to my students have all conspired to keep me off the river for about two months. In that time, autumn has blown away, and winter has arrived in the Texas hills. I have not been well. I have begun to lose my way.

The river keeps me balanced, and over the past few months, I have felt that old familiar edge building inside me that threatens to pull me over. The peace of this journey has been receding. Old memories of dark places have begun to drift by my waking dreams. It is like when you are paddling your kayak down a gentle stream and you hear rapids ahead. Sometimes the universe is screaming at you, I am reminded. It's time to bend a rod, cast a weighted line, and let everything drift back into perspective.

The San Gabriel River flows some distance from my home, still within the Hill Country, although just barely so. It's not a place I normally go because there is so much good fishing closer to home, but it has been on my to-do list of places to explore. The San Gabriel flows just south of Fort Hood, the place where so many soldiers have walked onto airplanes to fight in distant lands for reasons that were not always clear. They have faced their fears of uncertainty with more grace than seems common or expected. Some never come home. Others come home in broken pieces that will never be whole again.

Many, as I once did, find themselves wondering if breathing is all it's cracked up to be. I can tell them that it is. They must continue to breathe, but they must not try breathing indoors for a while. They must go to the rivers and streams and sit on large rocks watching the way leaves float by. They must let the ringing in their ears be carried away by the sound of pure rushing water. They must let go in order to find themselves once more. They must reject the broken spirit they were given by life's events and regain the whole spirit with which they began. As Papa Hemingway wrote, "Man was not meant for defeat. He can be destroyed, but never defeated." I know I have stood in the Big Two-Hearted River of my own landscape and it, and mayflies, and rainbows . . . saved me. These things will save you, too.

I was driving into the morning sun on the December day that I went to meet the San Gabriel. Just north of Johnson City, the landscape begins to lay down with hills rolling like waves in the sea. It is still the Hill Country, although this portion of it is called the Lampasas Cut Plains. I don't know why; they aren't plains, just hills that seem far less ambitious than those I am used to. So, as I drive out of Johnson City—which isn't a city—into the Lampasas Cut Plains—which aren't plains—I find myself feeling less and less at home.

Here the mountain cedar trees seem more like bushes and the oaks get fewer and smaller. The hills open into wide, rolling expanses, and overall, I can almost feel the vibe of Austin reverberating from the east.

I watch for a Prius covered in pink bumper stickers or Volvos with "love beads" hanging from the rearview mirror, and seeing none, I remain calm and carry on. A man in a rusted pickup truck with his rifle in the rack overhead tips his hat to me as he drives by. I feel more at home and wave back to him as if to say, "Thank you, neighbor." We Texans make eye contact and greet each other, even when traveling at seventy miles per hour. I hope we never lose this habit.

Meeting a river for the first time feels like a first date. You're always hopeful but try not to come into it with high expectations. In this case, my plan was to meet the river where the north and south prongs come together to form the San Gabriel main branch. This meeting of two streams happens within the northern limits of Georgetown. If you've read this far, you may know by now that I'm a fly-fisher and backwoodsman who desires solitude. Towns and traffic are not my idea of fun. Still, I had heard that Texas Parks and Wildlife had dropped about 1,000 stocker rainbows into the San Gabriel at this point. And after a week of freezing temperatures, I knew the bass would not be biting farther upstream. Also, I wanted to see the origin of the main river before it rolls out of the hills and into the central plains.

Driving into Georgetown, I kept crossing the north and south branches as they tumbled over rocks and wound their way toward the place where they both become one river. I parked beneath a massive sycamore tree and walked up to the water's edge. There was a small bridge where a flock of mallards quacked their displeasure upon my arrival. Walking out onto the bridge, I could see where the two streams met and formed the main branch of the San Gabriel. The fast water of both narrow branches quickly dissipated into a slow, deep, wide river. Looking a quarter mile down, I could see why the river changed its tempo . . . a dam.

On my side of the river was a lovely park space with ancient cypress, sycamore, and pecan trees along with a walking trail. There was ample space to backcast. It was very cold, and a strong wind blew behind me as I walked along the river looking for structure or any sign of rising fish. I made a mental note: Good, strong backcasts will lead to easy forward casts.

I could hear traffic in the distance. This would normally be enough to make me leave, but it was a beautiful, cold December day, and I had shown up determined to know that river just as it is, not as I wished it to be. The air was crisp and cold, the sun shining, and I planned on casting to stocker rainbow trout and accepting them as they were as well. I don't disrespect stockers as others do. Yes, there is something more special about catching wild native fish, but stockers can still teach me things about life. Like us, they live with the illusion of forever.

After walking to the dam and back, I strung up my rod while still considering the river. A limestone cliff formed the opposite bank. The river was too wide for me to be able to cast any farther than halfway across, even with this tailwind. I tied on a black size 10 Olive Bead Head Woolly Bugger and slowly walked back down toward the dam, watching the water as I walked. Just below the dam, the river became wild again with tailwater-specific aquatic vegetation and a complex run of pocket water. I knew the trout were above the dam but made a mental note to return to this river after the water warmed in the spring. It was a beautiful spot, and for a moment, I was missing Megan, my daughter and best fishing buddy.

At first, I just stood there with the cold December wind at my back watching the river spill over the top of the dam. Birds were singing in the branches of the sycamores and the pecan trees while flocks of mallards paddled by me like so many feather boats. I could hear them calling to each other across the wide expanse of water, and they seemed happy. I felt happy too.

Applying power into my backcast, I was able to send amazing forward casts into the river, making me look better than I am. It felt good, casting, stripping in line, and recasting. Oversized sycamore leaves floated down into the water, and at least in that moment, the San Gabriel seemed magical. Any tension I had earlier simply drifted with the leaves . . . downstream and over the dam. Perspective, all that matters, and all we ever have, is the moment we are within.

Working my way slowly up the river, I just settled into the rhythm of casting. Casting is meditation. It's like following your breath to quiet your mind, except when I have tried this in the past, my mind seldom shuts up. When I'm on a river or small stream casting toward brightly colored fish, my mind is always at peace. I suspect my breathing and heartbeats all move at the same tempo as a Texas Hill Country spring creek.

Partway back toward the confluence of the north and south prongs, I came across a series of springs, each lined by stone walls that funneled fresh spring water into the San Gabriel. At some points, stone steps had been built so that you could walk down about six feet into the ground and see the clear, cold water bubbling out of the limestone and then tumbling across jumbled rocks to the river. Just inside the outlet of one of these springs, there was a plunge pool where I could see a good-sized largemouth bass holding in the current. Stupidly, I tried a clumsy cast of a streamer into the pool and immediately spooked what turned out to be a half-dozen bass. The cold had made me careless. I made a mental note to rest this spot and come back for a stealthier attempt.

It would have been nice to catch some of the trout in the main channel, but I didn't, and in fact, I saw no sign of their presence even though I knew they were present. The water below the dam and above the joining of the two smaller and wilder branches of the San Gabriel had the same clarity I am used to from Hill Country streams. But the water just above the dam had that deep darkness I've seen on the Blanco and San Saba where the hand of humanity has come in to "fix things." In each such location, organic detritus builds behind the dam, and over time, the river suffers.

The day remained windy and cold, but the sun was bright, and I had the river space mostly to myself. As cold as it was, I was surprised to find turtles sunning themselves by the dozens on every rock and fallen tree. Even on this frosty December morning, small blue wildflowers bloomed along the riverbank. After reaching the bridge with nary a single strike, I worked my way back to the spring-fed pool where the bass were suspended, as if in molten glass or some ancient amber. It was beautiful.

There was a crumbling stone wall near the spring, and I used it as cover as I spied the pool. I crouched down behind the wall, partially protected from the icy wind, watching the pool. This, too, is a Zen-like experience. Whenever I simply sit and watch, in time, the world becomes clearer, and in fact, I see. The water was moving quickly down from the spring and out into the river channel, but the pool was tranquil. One by one, each bass began to appear to me; they were always there, of course . . . I was simply blinded by the noise in my head. Silence and solitude bring clarity.

After sitting motionless at the spring for some time, I was able to find a half-dozen good-sized largemouth bass that were holding in the pool. I decided that I'd have only one chance at them and that a stealthy downstream cast was in order. The pool was too shallow, narrow, and too clear for a streamer. Whatever fly I selected had to land softly on the up-current side so that only the fly and the tippet would be visible to the bass.

I must have looked funny to the few people who walked along the river trail as I worked my way around and planned my cast. The degree of difficulty was this: a strong, icy crossing tailwind; two sycamore trees and a pecan; crystal-clear, fast-moving water; and the very finite limits of my casting skill. I chose and tied on a size 12 elk hair caddis just because it's a bug that pops up everywhere. Waiting for a slight break in the wind, I drew back and let slip a surprisingly well-placed bounce cast. The fly drifted in front of two good-sized bass, then past them to the next, and with the leader still slack, it went onward to the last two. Nothing! I even tried skittering the caddis across the water on the third try, which just spooked them. I'm almost sure they looked at me with the expression of, "Are you kidding? It's freezing! We're not eating anything!" After another try and then a third, I reeled in, determined to return on a warm day.

After breaking down my rod and putting away all my gear, I walked back to the river and just stood there, taking it all in. It really didn't matter that I didn't catch any fish. I caught what I really came for: peace, perspective, and healing. Most of all, this wasn't a wasted day. So many days that I will never be able to get back have been wasted doing the things other people think I should be doing. So many hours, days, weeks, months, and, yes . . . even years have been wasted in an office trying to "make a living." As the Clint Eastwood character Josey Wales once said, "Dying ain't a good way to make a living."

Wild streams and fish are a medicine that I have used and have prescribed to others. As a supporter of Project Healing Waters Fly Fishing, I have seen firsthand how powerful the magic of the rivers can be. Working in partnership with Heroes On the Water and the Guadalupe River Chapter of Trout Unlimited, fly fishermen and kayakers have been able to help wounded warriors make the transition from the military to civilian life as well as act in support of their physical therapy process.

During one visit to the Center for the Intrepid in San Antonio, I had the honor of acting as the left arm of a soldier who had lost his own in Iraq to an improvised explosive device. While his wife looked on, I helped as he tied a Clouser minnow. The physical therapist explained to him how he would soon learn to use his new prosthetic arm and would be tying his flies without any help. While elements of fly-fishing such as tying and practice casting across the lawn helps wounded warriors with their physical therapy needs, actual time on the water is healing. In my own way, I know of what I speak. When your mind wages warfare within you, peace can be found within a streamside pool.

Fly-fishing contains within it the power to promote understanding. If all that our children ever know is a virtual world, then the real world will be allowed to die, and when it stops breathing, so do we. If fly-fishing were applied to working with kids of the inner city or who are beginning to drift "into the system," perhaps we could see a reduction in the "pipeline to prison." And, through responsible, ethical hunting, fishing, and other participative outdoor activities, we might be able to create the next generation of actively engaged and effective conservationists.

Relationships, like gardens, must be cared for. You can't just plant them and walk away. Americans are losing touch with real nature, and in doing so, we lose touch with our own true nature. We only save that which we love, and we only love that which we know.

Sometimes, dead faces haunt me. They flash before my eyes, and I know they will never really go away. Seeing the best and worst of humanity changes you. It makes you mortal. It keeps you humble. You know what it is like when life leaves someone's eyes. You know these things, and you can never manage to unknow them. They are the things you carry.

I remember a young US Marine crying in my office, wondering if he would ever be whole again. I told him that he was having a normal reaction to an abnormal experience. He seemed relieved. There have been many after him who have found the same relief in a few words and in simple kindness.

I remember the young soldier I sat and talked with at the Center for the Intrepid in San Antonio. I was there as a volunteer for Project Healing Waters. He was there because his legs were both blown off in Afghanistan. He told me how he would never see the enemy, and how one by one each of his best friends were killed or maimed by improvised explosive devices, until it was his turn.

He sat there with no legs below the knee, and I could see in his eyes that he felt guilty. He told me that he was trying to get the Army to keep him and that all he wanted was to go back to his unit . . . over there. Then he said, "Does that sound crazy?" He lowered his head and said, "I'm waiting to see the shrink now." I told him, "Pick up your head soldier. You did your part and more." Then I said, "It's not crazy . . . I'm in my fifties, and I still feel like a slacker because I'm not there. I served before you were born." He smiled.

Across from me was a beautiful young girl in camouflage BDUs. We smiled at each other. She was missing her right arm. I wanted to teach her how to cast with her left. Nature heals. Nick Adams taught me where to go for that silent peace. I knew why he couldn't stand the idea of ever using another salamander as bait. I knew. I still know, and I will never forget.

As I drove back through the Hill Country, all the thoughts I had come to the river to lay aside returned to me. All the questions left unanswered remained. Perhaps the answer to each isn't a solution to any of them. Like a Humphrey Bogart character, I could never stand by and let injustice happen no matter how much I wished to fight no more.

My dear friend Lieutenant Colonel Dave Grossman spoke of the three types of people: sheep, wolves, and sheepdogs. I was born a sheepdog. I was born a "rough" man, bred to protect the sheep from the wolves. Still, each time I connect to a fish, I bring him in quickly and keep him in the water as much as possible and release him gently. Kindness is not species-specific.

When you've known human cruelty, you crave loving-kindness. When you've known conflict, you desire peace. When you've seen cowardice and apathy, you become a disciple of courage and caring. Driving away from the San Gabriel, I knew that I will always stand up because I can't help myself. Still, if I had my choice, there would be no reason for sheepdogs. If I had my choice, I would not "want to be a god or a hero. Just to change into a tree, grow for ages, not hurt anyone."

CHAPTER SIXTEEN

Nueces

People walk away from perfectly good lives to make lots of money, only to end up spending all that money and more trying to buy back their old lives. My plan is to stay happy even if it fucking kills me.
~ *JOHN GIERACH*

THE NUECES IS A LONG WAY FROM MY LITTLE TOWN. IN DRIVING TIME, it takes about two hours to get there. It seems a world away from where I live on the edge of the Texas hills and the city that threatens to swallow them. Nueces Canyon reminds me of Montana. The floodplains of the river and the foothills surrounding it remind me of parts of Africa. It's not at all like the rainforests of West Africa where I spent almost two years of my life, but it reminds me of the Rift Valley in Kenya and the rolling thorn-scrub hills of northern Namibia.

Sometimes when I'm walking through these hills, I have visions of kudu, zebra, and elephants. Sometimes, as I drive through these hills, I do see many varieties of African and Asian wild-game animals. This is because the Texas Hill Country is a near-perfect habitat match for many of the antelope species of Africa, and ranchers have taken to raising them in large, high-fence operations. Nowhere is this truer than along the grassy bottomlands of the Sabinal, Frio, and Nueces Canyons.

I have lived and traveled throughout Africa. Around my neck, I wear a silver chain, and from it, silver talismans are suspended. One of these talismans is in the shape of Africa. I had it custom made in the Ivory Coast by an Ashanti gold- and silversmith from Ghana. I have worn it every waking hour of every day since 1984. Suspended from the walls of my writing room are the images of the animals I hunted in Africa. Each day, I look up at the full-shoulder mounts of kudu, gemsbok, hartebeest, and springbok, along with the tusks of the old warthog I took along the Angolan border and the hide of my Kalahari zebra. Pieces of rose quartz, iron ore, petrified wood, and tourmaline are strewn across my desk, all reminders of great adventures.

Africa gets under a man's soul. She's like a sensuous woman that you once met, and no matter how hard you try, you can't get her out of your mind. You remember her every detail. You remember her deep, inviting eyes and the texture of her skin, the sound of her voice, and how she smiled when you looked at her. You remember that casual flirtatious touch that told you that she wanted you to stay just a little longer or come back to her soon if you truly must leave her now, and how that brief moment of your touching made you wish that you did not have to leave her; and you lament the distance between you, and you curse fate for your rotten luck. I do not know if I will ever see Africa again, but in my dreams and in my mind, Africa will always be a part of me.

As I was driving along the Nueces near its headwaters above the tiny town of Vance, I first saw the herd of springbok grazing along the river. Then, looking beyond them and into the tree line, I saw two magnificent reticulated giraffes. The last time I saw these creatures was while on safari in the Meru District of Kenya. Yes, the Nueces River Valley can leave me dazed as if in a dream. Simultaneously, I watch African game grazing next to Texas white-tailed deer in front of hills that are so steep that they seem more like the foothill mountains of Montana.

This is a wide-open, deep-down, high-up sort of landscape. It is unique to the Texas hills, and no other part of the Hill Country looks like this. The Nueces Canyon feels wild. The Nueces River was another one of my "someday" places. Through the decades, I've said to myself that someday I'd make the long drive over there and fish it. This year was the year of putting the words "someday" behind me.

Driving from Vanderpool to Leakey and Campwood is an adventure. I know that this is called the Hill Country, and in most places, this name rings true. Still, the hills between Vanderpool and Campwood are steep and ear-poppingly high, and the road winds and twists menacingly along the sheer cliff's edge. A sign at each end of the road warns of how many people (mostly motorcyclists) have died on this road, and you realize that looking at the expansive scenery for more than a moment can lead to you becoming a permanent part of the canyon floor.

The Nueces is born way back in the northwestern hills between Vance and Hackberry, south of the town of Junction. Farther south of these headwaters, the landscape begins to open out toward the Devils River and the Chihuahuan Desert. Just to the west of here, the hills drift off into the Permian Basin where windmills generating power chop up migrating birds and where the right-of-way for the power lines has destroyed millions of trees and acres of wildlife habitat. I think they call this "green energy." I am a proponent of renewable energy sources, but it is also important to realize that everything we do impacts the environment.

To the northwest is the Llano Estacado. The name is derived from the Spanish words for "staked plains" because it was so vast, flat, and featureless that the explorers would have to drive wooden stakes into the ground to act as landmarks. Spanish conquistador Francisco Vázquez de Coronado crossed it in 1541. He described it as a "sea of grass," and he wrote, "I reached some plains so vast, that I did not find their limit anywhere I went, although I travelled over them for more than 300 leagues . . . with no more land marks than if we had been swallowed up by the sea . . . there was not a stone, nor bit of rising ground, nor a tree, nor a shrub, nor anything to go by."

Since then, much of the prairie has been replaced with cotton fields, and the bison have long since been eradicated. The Great Plains warriors of the Comanche Nation were not beaten by blue-coated invaders directly as much as their livelihood was eliminated by buffalo hunters, their horses were stolen by soldiers, and their world was turned upside down by everyone heading west. I guess that was their sad manifest destiny.

Perhaps this is the way of things. The Comanche pushed out the Apache and then were, in turn, pushed out by men from Tennessee with covered wagons and repeating rifles. Settlers from Germany, Czechoslovakia, and Poland settled in the Hill Country, and Mexicans migrated up to its southern limits along the Rio San Antonio. Together, they all became Texans except for the Comanche, who were forced to become Oklahomans.

Of all the travelers across this land, perhaps the First Nation Texans were the wisest. They seemed to know that when you come to a land, you should love it, learn it, and live within its arms. It is a foolish thing to begin the work of changing any place into that from which you have just run away. Wherever we go, there we are. We can't seem to run far enough to escape ourselves.

Of all the Hill Country landscapes, this stretch has the greatest opportunity for wild preservation and the reintroduction of lost native species. These hills used to be home to jaguars, mountain lions, black bears, coyotes, bobcats, and Mexican wolves. Now, all but the mountain lion, coyote, and bobcat have been exterminated.

On occasion, a black bear migrates into the hills from Mexico, and we know this because they are immediately shot by ranchers upon discovery. Not long ago, a young male black bear was sighted near Mountain Home, Texas, at the headwaters of the Guadalupe River. It was shot by a rancher who said that he felt threatened by the bear. There have been several claims of black bear sightings near Menard in the northern Hill Country, and although there has been no claim of anyone shooting them, it is their likely fate.

Mountain lions suffer a similar fate in Texas as they are not regulated as a game animal but rather treated as vermin. I am an ethical hunter, and I support the ancient ways of hunting, fishing, and ranching. Still, we must have some wild lands remaining in this nation. I am convinced that the only way this will happen is for organizations such as the Nature Conservancy, Western Rivers Conservancy, Trout Unlimited, and others to join forces with the US Department of the Interior and State Parks and

Wildlife Departments to purchase and conserve wild landscapes. Only this sort of unified commitment will save our wild places from becoming rooftop-covered eyesores. The Texas Hill Country deserves this kind of thoughtful commitment. I have nothing to offer it, but my voice.

—⊷⊶—

The first time I explored the Nueces River was in the late springtime. The wildflowers were still in full bloom, and while the steep, plunging hillsides were draped in deep evergreen, the roadsides and meadows were dotted in purple, blue, red, orange, and yellow. Prickly pear cactus burst into yellow-orange blooms, and the last globe-like, greenish-white antelope horns reached up toward any sunny roadside patch.

Spring in these hills erupts into hope, and in a loud voice, it says life, life, life! Everything fits here; everything is in sync. The scissor-tailed flycatchers arrive just as the insects hatch, and the hummingbirds and butterflies arrive just as the flowers bloom. The tadpoles fill the shallows just as do the newborn water snakes. Iridescent, multicolored dragonflies dip and hover as bass leap and spin, and if you listen, you can hear it all calling out—life, life, life, circular, spherical, life!

Vance is not a "town." Like so many spots of the map here, it is really a church, graveyard, and post office in the middle of vast ranchlands and wildscapes. This is a place where traditionally, as in most of the Hill Country, ranchers have suppressed natural fires and allowed longhorn cattle to graze and overgraze, and now the grasslands have slowly been lost to invading mountain cedar trees. This is ironic since the overgrazing and fire suppression lead to cedar invasion, and this, in turn, leads to ranchers spending money to eradicate excess cedar and artificially replenish the grassland. With the help of Texas Parks and Wildlife Certified Master Naturalists, more ranchers are learning how to balance the raising of livestock with the protection of native grasses, forbs, trees, soil, and water.

In the same way, some ranchers are learning the value of managing for native white-tailed deer and African exotics. As browsers, they have less impact on the grasses, and due to their increased value to paying hunters, they require less population density in order to be profitable. Preservation is only possible in the rare instance when we choose to exclude all human impact. Conservation happens when value is added to the function of protecting wildlife and habitat. In practical terms, we need conservation and education. Building win-win opportunities for native flora, fauna, and traditional private land use does more to save this landscape than all the petitions on the internet.

The Nueces twists narrow and wild through the game ranches just south of Vance. This is where I first stood at the river's edge. It is really a small stream at Vance, and sadly, the property owners had a single line of wire blocking the way and a "No Trespassing" sign posted on the nearby stream bank.

Legally, I had every right to fish this perfectly lovely stretch of newborn river. It was the perfect place for solitude. Whereas the Nueces opens wide farther downstream, here it meandered past a herd of African springbok and was young enough to roll-cast across at any point. Legally, I could have ducked under the wire, and if I never left the water or the line of the high-water mark along the shore, I was on state land, not private property. Still, Texans take privacy and home security in a serious way, and as a Texan, I respect that. And, as lovely as this spot was and as disappointed as I was about passing it by, it wasn't worth getting shot over. I drove south.

Passing through Campwood, I found a crossing where the river is wide and, in places, deep. There was a spillway from a small dam at the park just upriver, and as I waded into the cool, clear water, the sound of falling river filled my ears. It sounded nice, but I can always tell the difference between water that falls as humankind wishes it to fall and that which simply follows the pull of gravity and the natural rhythm of the landscape. I prefer the wild sounds and will take a singing warbler over any clucking chicken.

I began casting into a deep pool where about forty feet out I could see a limestone ledge just beneath the surface. After looking at the river for a while, I decided to try a 3X tippet leader with a size 10 Clouser that was tied with white and chartreuse bucktail and a bit of silver flash. The water here just looked "bassy" and screamed the word "streamer" at me.

After just a few good casts, my rod doubled over, and something biggish was pulling line and leader toward the current. I applied a little side pressure and moved it back into the pool, and then it was airborne, shaking its gaping big-mouthed, black-dotted, olive-sided self at me. The Guadalupe bass is not native to the Nueces River. These waters belong to native largemouth bass, and after a bit of a battle, I had a three-pounder in my landing net. He was glaring at me indignantly in the way that bass sometimes do, and I felt the sudden need to apologize and set him free quickly. I don't think he accepted my kind words. This old boy had attitude. I can respect that.

Two more casts and I was bringing in a small and then a tiny overachieving yellow sunfish. They just looked embarrassed, the way people do when they fall for a practical joke and hope no one they know noticed. I set them free and moved downstream to an area that reminded me of a Caribbean sand flat except the large, shallow expanse was over a solid fifty-yard-long, hundred-yard-wide slab of continuous limestone. About one to two feet of quick-moving clear water ran over the massive slab, and each edge dropped off into a pool that ranged from four to ten feet deep with a mixture of rock and waving green aquatic vegetation along the bottom.

Casting along the drop-off, I managed another hookup in short order, bringing in a yellow-bellied sunfish and then another largemouth in the one-pound range. I noticed how the submerged rock-line turned along the far edge of the river and cast toward that transition. I had settled into the casual rhythm of casting, letting my streamer swing into the current and stripping back without really paying attention as much as I should have been. It was right about then that the waters parted, and a bucket-mouthed monster inhaled the helpless Clouser. This fish could have eaten the last one in a single gulp. I was so shocked by the strike that I didn't set the hook properly, and with its first and only headshaking leap, this denizen of the semi-deep spit my fur and feather offering in my face.

I just stood there wondering what in the hell just happened. The biggest bass of my life just made a fool out of me. I was slack-jawed and looking embarrassed, the way people do when they fall for a practical joke and hope no one they know noticed. Looking back toward the bridge where I had parked my truck, I could see a border patrol agent parked, window down, watching in amusement.

I moved downriver away from inquisitive eyes so that I might undo the "Nazi knot" I'd managed to tangle into my leader. I call them "Nazi knots" because whenever I make one either in a tree limb or in the air, usually the result of some knee-jerk panic over a surprise fish . . . I envision a Nazi officer in his sharp, black uniform pointing a Luger at me. In the vision, the Nazi says menacingly, "Unless you want to be shot, you must make a single cast and manage a triple twist, double half-hitch around that tree limb while stumbling backward and completing a triple lutz, triple axel in the river and not looking." I couldn't do it if my life depended on it, but somehow I manage the most intricate tangles by accident. They really are works of art.

My next visit to the Nueces was with my best fishing buddy, my daughter Megan. I was so excited about the vast, open canyon and steep hills of the Nueces that I couldn't wait to show this place to her and share the river, building more memories. The past is worthless except for those memories that bring a smile to our face. I love to rewind those movies. All the rest of what happened in life should end up on the editing floor or be set adrift on the currents.

It was early autumn now, and the river was running deep. The sky was slate-gray with low clouds, and a light mist hung in the air. It had the effect of rendering the great vistas I had witnessed on my first trip invisible. Still, each place has its charms in every season and every mood.

The wind was briskly blowing into our faces. I noticed that this seems to be a theme on this wide expanse of river. The wind comes down from the distant hills that look like mountains and blows with authority upriver. The power of the steady wind causes a strange effect, whereas the current is running southeast and the top-water chop is blowing northwest. I was cool, perhaps too cool, and although the water was clear as usual, the lack of sunlight made sight-casting impossible. I was reminded of those times on a turtle-grass flat where the clouds block the sun and the choppy surface makes it near impossible to see the bonefish unless they tail-up.

An osprey flew overhead, watching and waiting for something to happen. He called out to us, one fisherman to another. I said, "Good morning," as we made eye contact. Then, flying low over the water, a belted kingfisher passed me by. He didn't look back. Still, we all had the same idea, although I'm sure every time I release a fish, they wonder what I'm thinking. Have I evolved or devolved? Either way, I had no opportunity to explain that there are simply too many humans on Earth and not enough osprey and kingfishers.

Megan caught the first fish, and I always hope that this will be the case. Each time we fish together, I hold a silent hope the first and biggest fish are hers. This day, all my hopes came true. I stopped fishing and just watched her play whatever she had a hold of. Her six-weight was bent over like a divining rod pointing the way to something powerful. Whatever it was, it pulled hard enough to be a bass but fought in the slab-sided way that yellow-bellied sunfish do, using the current to their best advantage. It took a while for us to see that she had the biggest sunfish I've ever seen. It would fill the average frying pan with no room for fried potatoes. He had that beautiful egg-yolk yellow color to his breast and handsome olive-colored sides. She slid him back into the river, and we hugged and smiled at each other broadly, another memory made.

It was on my next cast that I felt what amounted to more of a tick on my line than an actual strike. My rod-tip vibrated, and I stripped in the line. At the end of my tippet dangled the tiniest sunfish I've ever seen. He was only slightly bigger than the size 10 woolly bugger I was tossing. Megan and I laughed at the irony as I put him back into the river.

───

It was after Christmas when I finally made it back to the Nueces. Throughout the late autumn days when water temperatures were still warm enough for bass, I kept telling myself that I had plenty of time to get back out to the Nueces and chase big bass. By December, the Hill Country had experienced a month of freezing temperatures, wind, and rain, and all of this conspired to keep me indoors.

Even though I don't live in a cabin, I get cabin fever, or what John Gierach calls "the shack nasties." I finally broke down and made it out to the tailwater section of the Guadalupe and caught a few trout just to keep my sanity, but all my bass fishing spots were too frosty to be anything other than a chance to get wet. Then I saw the seven-day "forecast" with a scientific prediction of sunshine and warm temperatures, and I knew that would be my one chance to revisit the Nueces.

When I crossed the steep hills and descended into the canyon, it was like driving into Hogwarts. A low, black ceiling of clouds hung from the edges of each hilltop, and the wind blew hard and icy-cold. I could have made a better prediction using some feathers and chicken bones. It didn't matter, I was going fishing.

When I finally arrived, I suited up and stepped into the river at the same bridge just south of Campwood. Looking back, I saw the same border patrol vehicle parked, and I'm sure he or she was wondering what kind of nutcase was standing in the river on a windy, cold day waving a stick. The first thing I noticed when wading through the luxurious, green aquatic vegetation and the clear, clear, cold water was a deer's head floating in the shallows. Someone had cut it off and hacked off the antlers. I moved farther downriver to one of my favorite spots, the same spot where I caught the three-pound largemouth in the springtime. Looking across the limestone flats, I saw the bloated body of the aforementioned deer. I could smell it, too. *Lovely*, I thought.

Slowly, methodically, with Zen-like inner silence, I fished each section of the river in the eye-watering, windy, frigid winter air knowing all along that I wasn't going to catch anything. I was outdoors on the river. Nothing else really mattered. I had solitude and felt at peace. When I finally took my last cast, I reeled in and said to myself aloud, "I waited too long." My father used to say, "He who hesitates is lost." Right again, Dad!

Little by little, I'm buying my life back. I invest in life each day. We should never allow ourselves to end up standing alone in the cold thinking, *I waited too long*. There is no such thing as "someday." There is only this moment, only this day. Life happens. It isn't bad or good, it just is. Each of us can either look out the window wishing we could live, or we can go out the side door and just go do it. My plan is to live a happy and full life . . . even if it fucking kills me.

CHAPTER SEVENTEEN

Headwaters

*Everything the Power of the World does is done in a circle. The sky
is round, and I have heard that the earth is round like a ball and
so are all the stars. The wind, in its greatest power, whirls. Birds
make their nests in circles, for theirs is the same religion as ours. The
sun comes forth and goes down again in a circle. The moon does the
same, and both are round. Even the seasons form a great circle in
their changing and always come back where they were. The life of a
man is a circle from childhood to childhood, and so it is in everything
where power moves.*

~ BLACK ELK, AS QUOTED BY JOHN G. NEIHARDT

THE HEADWATERS OF EACH HILL COUNTRY RIVER SEEM CHILDLIKE.
There is an innocence about the way they bubble up from limestone
springs and meander under the trees carrying leaves and mayflies like it's
nobody's business. I like that, it feels right. After decades of spilling out
where society drains me, I'm ready to go home. It's counterintuitive how
complicated it is to make life simple again.

The first step is to stop thinking and begin to understand the wrongness of complexity. Life is simple, and we need to keep it that way. The second step is to start letting go of things, including expectations. I've been giving away my "stuff" like a dying man. I've given away everything that I don't need or use, including furniture, pots, pans, dishes, clothes, and three truckloads of books. I have let go of unreasonable expectations and have learned to take life in stride. The boy I once was is far wiser than the man I've allowed myself to become. It's time to go backward until I find the original me, back at the headwaters of being alive.

I know that I'm not alone in my aloneness. There are others who are reading these words and are wondering, "What am I doing following such an unhappy path while my lifetime bleeds out of me?" And yet, we get back in that saddle each day and cross that empty, soulless life-scape, making a living while failing to live. Why?

When I stand in the headwaters of a Hill Country stream, it's like seeing a picture of a younger me, before the expectations of self and others began to crush my spirit. Living like that isn't living. It's the difference between being a reservoir and a lake; one lives naturally as it should while the other exists so that it can be slowly drained as the water-brokers see fit. Life should meander, not drain.

I remember buying my first fly-rod. It was an inexpensive, whippy fiberglass stick, but I was proud of it. That was the year after I left the Marine Corps, and Alice and I had moved to Montana. It was my first time in life going from door to door trying to find work. One business manager in Missoula looked at my résumé and half-listened to my presentation about my transferable skills of leadership, problem-solving, communications, planning, and logistics. And then he looked at me and said, "Sorry, I don't need anyone killed today." My heart sank. At that moment, I began to recall the stories of my Marine Corps mentors of being spat upon by college students as they returned from the hell that was Vietnam.

How many of our young troops will face this same fate? In the end, I never had the chance to use that first rod. I returned it for the money so we could afford to eat. It was like having to return a puppy to the pound. It was a sad day.

A year prior, I was a highly respected US Marine with a top-secret security clearance protecting heads of state and working in counterterrorism. Then, almost as if I had become another person, nobody wanted me. This was the beginning of a long journey home. It has taken me three decades to reach this point. Better late than never. Life unfolds. You can't force it.

⌁

There is something special about the headwaters, the place where each river is born. It somehow feels wilder, more pristine, and even, perhaps . . . innocent. These are the places less trampled by humanity. The birds sing with less care, the deer watch without running, water snakes lay motionless regarding me as I do them, and everything reminds me of when I was wilder, unscarred, unburdened by expectations and, in that way, perhaps, more primal. When I'm fishing the headwaters more than anywhere, I miss those days. I miss being that me. I miss being the boy who lived close to the Earth.

I remember when green lizards used to look me straight in the eye. The first one to do that was in the courtyard of the oldest house in America. It was an old Spanish house in St. Augustine, Florida. He was bright green, and somehow, he managed to both blend in and stand out from the light-green leaves and deep-purple flowers of the bougainvillea vine. I was about seven years old then, and I remember that there was a group of adults in the courtyard with me. None of the adults noticed the green lizard, and he, in turn, paid no attention to them.

I remember that it felt as if we were having a private conversation, my lizard friend and me. He seemed to know that I was not going to hurt him, which, in and of itself, was an amazing act of trust. I'm quite sure he was aware that house cats and little boys can both be tough on little green lizards. Even so, we spent some time together, him looking at me and me looking at him. I was sad to say goodbye.

When I was a very young boy, being out in nature was always my salvation, and nothing much has changed. Now in my fifties, when the world seems to close in around me, I always return to my Texas Hill Country. I walk along the limestone paths, past deer and golden-cheeked warblers, and I cast my line into a river, and as if by magic, the world melts away. Still, some things have changed. I have changed.

Somehow, over time, I began to become one of the adults who do not see the bright-green lizard, and to whom the lizard pays little attention. I have been the lesser for this change. It is not who I truly am; it is who I have allowed myself to become. I wandered off the path and onto the concrete. I became lost, but now, I'm going home. I'm returning to my homewaters.

When I was a young boy, many things used to look me in the eye. Deer would stare through the branches, barred owls from the oak trees, and garter snakes from the grassy creek beds. When we "grow up," all these spirits seem to drift out of our lives. We no longer see them, and they, in turn, sense that we are foreigners, existing in some dimension outside of the natural world. We hurry through that space in time that we all pretend to understand. We exist in the illusion created by our minds and accept the tribal lie as truth.

Chronologically, I am getting older with each passing day. Folks call it middle age, but that is also a lie because almost no man lives to be 103. Things begin to change for a man in this part of life. If he has any sense of self, soul, and spirit, he cannot help but notice. He sees his life slipping away like a leaf floating down a Hill Country stream. His life rushes and spills over the limestone and under the cypress trees. He can see the birds in the sky and the fish in the stream, but they are both worlds apart from the leaf and where it is going. The leaf will sink to the bottom and join the many pieces of the stream. In time, these silent souls come to life again. Fresh leaves of springtime shade the stream and hold the birds in the palm of their hands. This will happen no matter if a man pays attention or not; it is the way of things.

I have learned that much of what seemed so important in the past was like building something with blocks of air. I have learned that the agenda of the world, of society, is a selfish and foolish one. It seems that the world knows very little about living. Still, there is a price to be paid for paying attention. If you choose to blend with the leaves and enjoy the flowers, you must accept that the grown-ups will no longer accept you.

I have been paying attention more and more each day. I have noticed that as I pay attention, the little boy is finding his way home. These days, green lizards are looking me in the eye more often. I have noticed that the more I am present in the moment, without the clutter and noise of adulthood, the more authentically I am living. The trees seem greener, the breeze cooler, the rain more welcome, and people are naked and ridiculous in their self-importance. I think I'm growing younger.

———

The morning glow over the hills seemed reassuring. The road meanders and winds as the river did from Kerrville to the tiny town of Hunt. We drove around the towering limestone cliffs once carved by the same soft river. Sometimes, when the rains fall heavy, hard, and long upon the hills, the river changes everything all at once and cypress and sycamore trees fall to their doom while limestone boulders the size of hippos are tossed like marbles in some cosmic game of the gods. Most times, the river changes things slowly, imperceptibly, so that if you could live forever you wouldn't notice that the canyon wasn't there just a moment ago. Rivers are magical like that, sort of like canyons.

The headwaters of the Guadalupe are found at crossings with wonderful names like the following: Bumble Bee, Mystic, Panther Creek, and La Casita. The last crossing is called Dry Crossing, and it is dry. Here, the river lives under the stone, and the fish live not at all. We stopped at an unnamed crossing where a waterfall tumbles over rocks and roots and the river takes a lazy bend around massive, old cypress trees.

Megan took the first pool at the base of the waterfall, and I stripped out some line above it where a man-made dam creates another pool. Walking up to the water's edge, I watched as a half-dozen big carp moved along the dam and then on toward the deepest part of the pool. For a while, I just enjoyed the rhythm of the slow casting stroke demanded of me when loading my flexible fiberglass rod in the air. My stealthy green line slid out of the guides and onto the water that was still too cool for truly productive catching but just fine for truly enjoyable fishing.

After a while with no strikes, I reeled in my line and walked across the riffle, under the bridge, and around Megan, who was casting perfect loops into the plunge pool and toward the undercut distant bank. She smiled. I smiled too. Life was good. I have found things get easier once you learn to accept that, like the river does to boulders, sometimes life is going to move you to places you never imagined you'd be.

We had come to these headwaters before, a year ago, in the late summer. I walked over to the cove beneath the massive pecan tree, across from the ancient cypress trees, next to the large, flat rock from under which a three-foot garter snake, patterned like an old velvet curtain, slid away. My little glass rod bent behind me, slowing me down, bringing me home, and sending my line forward toward the fish.

Megan felt a few soft strikes but missed the hookup on each. I felt happy, and it didn't matter that the water was cold, the fishing slow, and the catching nonexistent. Standing next to the little waterfall with the sounds of cardinals and wrens in the air, nothing seemed to be missing in life.

It's easy for us to let life drift us too far downstream, away from our headwaters. If we're not careful, we forget where we came from or even who we are. The same is true of our connection or disconnection from the Earth. I still hold within me an overactive superego filled with unproductive religious guilt and unsettling American expectations, but now, I know how worthless all that baggage is and how it drags you down and deforms you, if you let it.

I guess, like the Dalai Lama, my religion is kindness. I'd have to toss a dose of courage in there and, finally, if I'm honest about it, there's an animist streak growing within me, not in the religious sense but rather in the childlike way I used to see life and spirit within everything. These days, I see life in roots and rocks, canyons and cardinals, stones and streams, wildflowers and white-tailed deer. These days, I see life in everything.

I love and value nature and the best of human nature. I feel gratitude and wonder whenever I consider the beautiful planet I call home. I see her as a part of me and me as a part of her. I can't bear for her to be harmed, left for dead, forgotten, unloved, unknown, undervalued. And that's what happens with distance. When we become distant from the Earth or each other, we lose our better nature. We lose such attributes as empathy, acceptance, understanding, respect, and caring. We begin to see each other as résumés and nature as a collection of resources. Neither is true. We are more than stardust and seawater. We can choose to be more.

"Everything the Power of the World does is done in a circle." With every circular looping cast, I reach back, reach forward, and up and down and make contact with now. Headwaters and lifetimes, both flow in circles. From raindrop, spring flow, streambed, seashore, cumulus cloud to snowflake . . . it's all connected. We're all connected. We're all in this together. Ram Dass was right when he said, "We're all just walking each other home."

CHAPTER EIGHTEEN

Homewater

In the depth of winter, I finally learned that within me there lay an invincible summer. And that makes me happy. For it says that no matter how hard the world pushes against me, within me, there's something stronger—something better, pushing right back.

~ ALBERT CAMUS

I HAVE NEVER CARED ABOUT BIRTHDAYS BEFORE. IT TOOK ME ONLY HALF a century to care. I have always cared about experiences, adventures, passions, moments, and, yes, even the feeling you get once you have overcome some great life-obstacle, some challenge that "they" said you could never conquer. I have made a lifetime hobby out of proving "them" wrong. I have never cared about anniversaries of birth or death before, but this one was different because it contained within it the celebration of joy and, behind it, the shadows of sorrow.

With each cast of my soft, amber-glass fly-rod, I heard voices . . . some were mine, and some were of those people for whom I hold a place in my heart, always. My Marine brother Dave's Lakota spirit animal, the red-tailed hawk, flew overhead calling down to me. I smiled and said, "Hello, Dave, I'm so glad you could be here." Megan was casting and catching bright green and black Guadalupe bass and bright green and yellow sunfish, and we each smiled at each other every time we set another fish-spirit free. Sometimes I just watch her cast, and as I do, I remember her standing in that same spot so many years ago. In my mind, I watch her grow up and older . . . years passing with each new forward loop. It's bittersweet. It's how life tumbles ever forward, like a river.

We decided on a downstream approach, wading past the shallow riffles by the Pooh Bear Bridge, and then around the little island where the deer tend to sleep. We split up as we do, about fifty feet apart, me at the first little jumble of stones, and Megan at the second. I always give her the second spot because traditionally, it is the lucky spot, and some good-sized bass often lurk in the shadows of the big cypress trees.

This time, I caught the first fish. It was the first fish I had ever caught with my new, little amber rod, and it bent over and vibrated as glass tends to do as the smallish Guadalupe bass jumped and jived among the rocks and riffles. Soon I had him at my side, slipped out the hook, and sent him on his merry way. *Thank you*, I thought, *Happy birthday to me!* I looked over at Megan, and she was smiling ear to ear. I saw that she was so happy for her battered father and his pretty little glass rod.

We spent the next hour or so leapfrogging past each other, working our way downstream, casting to the eddies and lies, under deep-cut banks and the occasional pocket or pool. Megan caught a few yellow-bellied sunfish and then hooked into a big Guadalupe bass that might have gone two pounds, but it slipped free before I could get to her with the net. We called it a long-distance release.

I worked my way along the undercut bank just enjoying the slow rhythm of casting glass. The sun was filtering through the cypress trees at that magical angle where everything feels golden. The bite was on, and we both took turns catching sunfish and bass at a steady rate until we came to the waterfall pool. Then, it seemed as if a switch had been flipped, and although the casting was lovely in this beautiful little pool, the catching had ended.

I let Megan work the main pool above the falls, and I stood carefully at the top casting across the deep plunge pool below. I looked back to watch Megan cast, and while I was paying attention to her, the current was twisting my leader around a submerged tree at the base of the falls. I broke it off, and we just looked at each other smiling. It had been a perfect morning on our homewater. It really couldn't get any better. We didn't need to utter a word. She snipped the fly off her line, and we both reeled in our lines. Tucking our rods backward under our arms, we began walking upstream toward the Pooh Bear Bridge.

As we walked back, both of us taking in the beauty of the river and the day, my best fishing and adventure buddy took my hand and said, "Happy birthday, Dad." I couldn't stop smiling. I had been losing my resolve with the anniversary that came before this one. A few days prior was the one-year marker of the day I drove home without my job, after so much betrayal, after so much loss far beyond a mere paycheck and benefits. It had been a journey of decades that tumbled and tore and wrenched away my core of beliefs, hopes, and illusions. Yet when I drove home that day, I did not feel anything, nothing at all. I was silent inside, not hollow, just silent, that's all. I had no plans except to fish and write and heal and, ultimately, to live.

When the one-year marker struck, I began to wonder, *Will this work?* I began to question, *Will anything I do or write ever matter? Do I have a life mission anymore?* But then, at that moment, walking hand in hand into the current of our homewater, it all came to me as clear and as true as a Hill Country stream. I was happy . . . truly happy. What comes next, we can never know, but on this day, and each day since the moment that my life path changed, I have been living not the dreams of another but rather the dreams of my own making.

Recently, I was watching an episode of the old classic series *North-ern Exposure*. I love that show and its wonderful imaginary town and its wonderful imaginary people, all of which seem all too real, or at least, I wish they were. In this episode, Chris, the deep-thinking and spiritual ex-convict radio announcer, decided that he was inspired to build a catapult, and as an act of performance art, he planned to toss a cow into the air and then have a town barbeque, with the aforementioned bovine as the "guest of honor." Once he finds out that the characters of Monty Python had already come up with the idea of catapulting a cow, he becomes despondent, feeling that his inspiration led him nowhere special.

And then, the pretty bush pilot Maggie's cabin burns down, leaving behind only a pair of shoes and a charred piano. In that moment, Chris is suddenly reenergized. The entire town turned out and cheered with joy as Chris's catapult launched Maggie's broken piano into the air, where it sailed in slow motion toward its crashing, cataclysmic destruction.

Maggie was free of her lost past now, it was gone, not mourned but rather let go of in a grand, arcing loop of liberating destruction. Quoting Pablo Picasso when he said, "Every act of creation is first an act of destruction," Chris shares with the smiling townsfolk what he had learned during his creative journey. "It's not the thing that you fling that counts, it's the fling itself."

"Every act of creation is first an act of destruction." As I stowed away my rod while watching the river drip from me toward the earth, those words swirl past my legs like the answer to my life's question. Those moments and loves most refreshing in life must be carried in our hearts. Those spirits that seek to define and limit us must be flung into the air where their own dark gravity reduces them to elements, now harmless.

Eckhart Tolle once wrote, "When your sense of self is no longer tied to thought, is no longer conceptual, there is a depth of feeling, of sensing, of compassion, of loving, that was not there when you were trapped in mental concepts. You are that depth." There is peace within the bending of the rod, and the laying of the line upon the water, and the natural rhythm of the river. These waters are "the root of the root" for me, and they carry me, and I carry them within my heart. Homewaters, take us home.

CHAPTER NINETEEN

Tailwaters

So, friends, every day do something that won't compute. . . . Give your
approval to all you cannot understand. . . . Ask the questions that have
no answers. Put your faith in two inches of humus that will build
under the trees every thousand years. . . . Laugh. Be joyful though you
have considered all the facts. . . . Practice resurrection.

~ WENDELL BERRY

THERE IS A TAILWATER FISHERY AT THE BASE OF CANYON DAM ON THE
Guadalupe River. The lower Guadalupe River is the southernmost trout
fishery in the United States. I envisioned the dam as being something
like the pictures I've seen of Hoover Dam, and the river was wide and
open so that beautiful looping casts could be made to undercut banks
where brown and rainbow trout were waiting for me. I pictured that
when I went there, a cool winter chill filled the air, and mayflies were
coming off the water just for me and the trout. As might be expected, it
was not at all as I expected.

⟨⟩

I had stayed up late at night on Christmas day. I was reading Peter Matthiessen's wonderful book *The Snow Leopard*. Then, falling into sleep around midnight, I awoke at 3:33 a.m. feeling deeply troubled and knew that I was not getting back to sleep. I was at the point in the story where he is wondering if he would die in the mountains and considering the question, "Why is death so much on my mind when I do not feel I am afraid of it?—The dying yes, but not the state itself. And yet I cling—to what? What am I to make of these waves of timidity, this hope of continuity, when at other moments I feel free?" I could have written those words, or at least, I wish I had.

John Gierach once wrote, "I get sentimental about small streams." That's me . . . I'm a sentimental sap when it comes to these little Texas streams. I worry about them. I think that's called love. Love is a powerful force. It moves us and connects us to other souls and streams and sunrises. By the time I came to the tailwaters, it was the winter trout season in the Texas hills. The day after Christmas was also my father's eighty-first birthday.

When I woke that morning in the blinding blackness of predawn, I wondered if I would ever see my father again. (As it turned out, I never did.) We talked on the phone at sunrise as I was driving to the river, and I told him that I was going to cast a line for rainbows in honor of him. He told me he was proud of me. It really doesn't matter if you're five or fifty, hearing something like that from your dad makes you feel good inside.

I'm proud of him too, and each time we spoke on the phone, I knew it might be the last. I guess I felt a little sentimental about that as well. I guess our lives have tailwaters too. They sort of spill out from under all the barriers and impediments and the things that drain away our spirit, and in the end, the victory is in remaining intact and authentic. We can't let anything drain the life out of us.

When I reached the river, the temperature had risen from thirty to forty-seven degrees. The water was very cold. I fished a dry fly downstream first and then a streamer, but the trout seemed to either be sleepy or they just found my antics to be amusing. I had risen before the sun and began the hour-and-a-half drive to the river early in hopes of being the first person to arrive. I was the second. Looking downriver at the pool that I had hoped to fish, I saw a lone fly fisherman standing there casting steadily into it. He wasn't catching anything either. Not wanting to crowd him and seeking my own solitude, I began working my way upstream, methodically tossing a streamer toward the far undercut riverbank.

There was a likely indentation in the riverbank between two massive cypress trees where the current swirled past and around the submerged limestone ridges. Casting across and letting the streamer swing into the current, I felt a massive tug and set the hook. The river exploded in rainbow flashes as he leaped into the air full of fury and fight. Tucking my rod between my legs, I used both hands to hold the big beautiful rainbow, slipping the hook free and sliding him back home. I guess he went a solid eighteen to twenty inches, not that it matters. It's nice to catch big, fat, healthy fish, but I love the little colorful ones just the same.

I turned upstream and fished the streamer and then later a copperjohn nymph upstream, again to no avail. Working my way up the canyon, I found two beautiful pools with a lovely section of rapids between them. Water dripped from the overhang of the limestone cliff, lesser sandpipers *kee-keed* over the water, and Spanish moss swayed from the arms of the cypress trees.

Everything looked like it was in sepia tone on account of it being winter, complete with gray skies and naked, gray-trunked cypress trees. There were a few trout rising to a sparse Trico hatch, but it was over before I could switch my leader and fly. That was okay, too; I like watching trout rise, even when I'm not catching them.

I found a perfect spot for lunch next to the two pools. Being a fairly good backwoodsman, I always know to take my time and just watch a river for a while. I kept hearing in my head the words of John Gierach, "You have a distinct advantage once you realize that you do in fact have all day." Sitting on a massive fallen sycamore tree log that was cleanwhite, divested of its bark, I had my lunch while watching the trout rising in the pools and listening to water tumble over the limestone riffles.

There is something about a simple lunch of a peanut butter and jelly sandwich and chocolate milk that just seemed to be fitting on the cold St. Stephen's Day . . . my dad's birthday. As I sat there watching the river,

I was also thinking about Dad. I was remembering him and his yellow fiberglass fly-rod that he bought at a hardware store because that's what you did back then when you had family obligations and very little money to spend on your own passions. I remember the big mason jar in which he had saved his pennies, nickels, and dimes so he could buy that rod and how excited he'd be as he and his buddy Charlie left home before sunrise to fish the headwaters for small brightly colored fish. Somehow, in all my moves around the world, I managed to lose the tip to my father's fly-rod. For years, I've lamented the loss and the fact that no matter how lovely my Winston 5 weight casts, I wanted to be able to feel the same feeling that my father had with his soft, yellow, fiberglass stick.

Recently, I came across an article in *Fly Fisherman* magazine by Cameron Mortenson entitled, "Fiberglass Revolution." Perhaps everyone else on this big blue ball already knew, but until that moment, I didn't know that fiberglass rods were making a comeback. As it turns out, I had a chance for redemption. From that article, I found two websites: Fiberglass Flyrodders and The Fiberglass Manifesto. A world of soft, slow, colorful rods came before my eyes. I may not be able to ever regain my father's rod, but I could come close.

When I first began to consider buying a glass rod, I heard the voice of guilt whispering into my ear; after all, I had gone from an executive salary with benefits to being a part-time professor without any insurance, financially or in life. My father's frugality kicked in along with the voices of all those Catholic nuns who told me to sacrifice myself for others, always. I began to wonder which outcome would bother me more, feeling like an idiot because I spent money on a rod that could have paid a bill, or feeling like a fool because I spent money on a bill that could have bought a lovely glass fly-rod. It was then that I decided that being an idiot was better than being a fool. I decided to search the narrow headwaters of my favorite Texas Hill Country rivers with a shorter, softer, fiberglass stick . . . just as Dad had done so very long ago.

At the third crossing of River Road along the lower Guadalupe is one of my favorite local fly shops: Action Anglers. I'd spent some time talking with the owner, Chris, about my meandering thoughts of enjoying a reflective experience in the headwaters of the Guadalupe, Llano, Medina, and Sabinal with a stick that is like my dad's. We also talked about my desire to explore the remote Devil's River and the usual talk about what bugs were on the water and the meaning of life. Chris is a soft-spoken, knowledgeable angler, and he's been very kind to me. Dave is there when Chris is not, and he and I have had some nice conversations about bamboo, bugs, and, of course, the meaning of life. I guess it's hard to fly-fish without catching a little philosophy along the way.

After lunch, I waded back out into the river, and just as it happened, an amazing slate drake mayfly hatch began to pop and sputter off the water. Trout began rising and then smashing the surface. I was ill-prepared. Looking into my fly-box, I realized, incredulously, I had come to the river without a single Adams fly—the simple solution to a size-12 Slate Drake hatch. The closest I could come was a Royal Wulff attractor pattern, which I began casting into the hatch and, in short order, watched as a twelve-inch rainbow danced on the water into my hands and then shortly thereafter, swam free again to rise another day.

When I set that lovely trout free, I thought of my dad when he was young, casting his cheap, yellow fiberglass rod toward little, wild brook trout. Looking across the water, I said to myself, *This one's for you, Dad.* After the hatch was over, I reeled in and began wading slowly downstream. It was another beautiful day to be alive. In fact, I'm not so sure that catching fish has all that much to do with it, although they are like salsa on an already magnificent meal.

When I was done thinking about Dad, I began thinking about Megan. Usually, fly-fishing quiets my mind. This was a morning and a day where I fished for a while and then watched the river flow by, neither of us in any big hurry. Sometimes I was focused on getting a good drift with a dry-fly or watching for movement on a nymph or methodically, rhythmically casting a streamer, and in those moments, I was perfectly thoughtless. Other times, I sat at the river's edge and just watched for rising trout, or singing wrens, or meandering memories.

Recently a friend said to me, "You think too much." I thought about that, and perhaps he's right. It may also be true that I feel too much, see too much, hear too much, and smell too much. I mean . . . most people never really notice the sounds of birds in the morning, the aroma of coffee, or the way pebbles on a streambed seem to reflect the colors of the universe. Most people forge right past those details. And most people don't wake up in the predawn black, black blackness, with eyes open into nothing, seeing everything. And finally, if I think about it, most people can't feel the spirit of a dear distant friend whom you have not seen in "forever" but still hold in your heart. I do. I'm odd that way . . . I think.

I've heard people say that we should live our life without regrets, and I suppose they are right, whoever "they" are, but I must admit to having a few regrets . . . and I regret that. Still, being an optimist, I treat my regrets like wandering thoughts that float into a meditative mind, I set them adrift, watch them float away, and bid them farewell.

If I let myself, I would regret lost love, friendship, experiences, opportunities, and all those times I've had to choose between this and that but wished for both. I won't do that because it's a waste of time that I can ill afford. Instead, I value the challenges and the obstacles overcome, the wounds survived, and the moments now held only in memory. The lines upon my battered face and soul are the texture of my story. No one gives a damn about blank pages. Only cowards fail to push the pen to page, and I'm afraid of cowardice.

When the hatch was over and the trout stopped rising, I tied on a streamer and worked my way down current. There is a pool under the bridge that I cast to, and in just a few casts, I connected to another pretty rainbow, this one perhaps a little bigger than the last but not by much. He flashed in the air and then in my hand, and as I released him back into the pool, I noticed how handsome a fish he really was.

I could see a few more twelve-inch trout holding along the submerged limestone in mid-river, but my attempts to entice them led to nothing, so I continued down to a pool just below a series of riffles. In a few casts, I hooked another twelve-inch stocker; this one didn't jump, he burrowed toward the deep bottom of the pool until I could bring him up. Once he was free, I looked upstream and saw that the trout were rising once more in a pool just above me. I couldn't see any bugs on the surface, and I wasn't prepared for the midges that probably were there yet unseen, so I tied on the smallest dry I could and walked around the pool so that I could try a downstream presentation. What this led to was some nice drifts and one clumsy attempt to set the hook that put every rising trout in the little pool sullenly down to the bottom. No matter. It was a beautiful pool, and the rising trout were magical.

Working back up toward the bridge with another black streamer, I casually cast to little plunge pools, limestone divots, and undercut banks. I tossed my line into a dark spot at the base of an old-growth cypress tree, and in an instant, my rod doubled over, and the fight was on. With the first leap, I could see I had my hands full. He was somewhere between eighteen and twenty inches long, thick and heavy shouldered, so much so, in fact, that at first, I thought I had a brown trout. Once I got him closer, I saw his lovely rainbow-spotted sides, and he jumped two more times before I could land him, and tucking my rod between my legs, it took both arms to hold him. As he slid back into the river, I just stood there for a while . . . smiling.

I felt lucky to be alive in this place. I thought of my darkest times and how they all led to this moment standing in this perfect tailwater listening to birds singing in the cypress trees. Had I ever given in to despair, this moment would never have been known. No matter what, life is worth living . . . all we must do is . . . keep casting.

I waded slowly upriver, back to the pool at the third crossing. I was going to just snip off the fly and let that last magnificent fish end my day, but I've never been good at quitting. Looking at the pool, I decided *"one more,"* and I cast upstream of its top edge, letting the black woolly drift and swing, and in that instant, I saw a flash and felt the tug and set the hook on another big leaping rainbow. He jumped once, twice, three times, and on that third leap, he landed headfirst into a pile of submerged branches that were wrapped around the bridge pylon. Half of the trout's body was underwater, and the tail end was flapping in the air.

I began to wade over to try and free him when I slipped into a deep hole and was smashed into the concrete pylon with such force that it knocked the wind out of me. I was suddenly up to my neck in rushing water and gasping for air, trying to work my way into the shallows. The fish was freed of both hook and branch by the sheer force of my impact, and as I struggled past the pain in my ribs and the power of the current, it swam peacefully away. Bent over in pain, I caught my breath. Looking up, I saw two anglers fishing the pool above me. I knew that they had witnessed the entire event, but they continued casting as if I were invisible, as if I were an apparition from some other dimension. Perhaps, I was.

—◦—

Megan and I began this journey together. And during the year, she chose a path and soon will leave for her next adventure. I sat there for a while and thought about that. After graduating with a degree in anthropology, she traveled to Peru as part of an archaeological research project near Arequipa. She worked in the Colca Valley, where she spent fourteen-hour days at 14,000 feet in elevation measuring ancient walls and identifying bits of ancient pottery. Like me, she has been dealing with uncertainty. Life has a way of changing our plans.

While in Peru, she learned how tough and resilient she could be and how much she loved the outdoors. Life happens as we plan. We all must fish the drift before us. So, after working hard and letting things just drift into place, my best fishing buddy will be moving on. This is as it should be. Love is always a key, never a cage.

I don't think I could ever find a fishing buddy as perfect for me as Megan. We are both there for the peace and beauty of it all and catching fish does not make or break any trip. I'm grateful for every moment we have shared on the river, and I know there are always new rivers for us to explore.

Unconditional love knows no limits; distance, time, and space change nothing.

A lot has happened since I began this new journey. I've been teaching part-time for one major Texas University already, and now, their rival has asked me to teach for them too, so ironically, I drive in one direction to teach students in the morning and another direction to teach students in the evening. One campus is in urban, downtown San Antonio, and the other is in the rural Texas Hill Country. The topics are identical, but the students are, in many ways, opposites.

In the morning, I teach inner-city students who are mostly Mexican American in origin. In the evening. I teach rural, ranch-raised students who are mostly of European American origin. The inner-city kids come from high-human-density, high-crime, lower-socioeconomic-level communities where drugs, gangs, and teenage pregnancy are rampant. The rural kids come from low-human density, low-crime, lower-socioeconomic-level communities where a connection to nature keeps most of them grounded, while trailer-park meth labs keep some of their parents high. I have met some of the most amazing young people in both worlds. In each case, it's up to each young person to make choices. And, in each case, it is up to us to give them that opportunity.

In his wonderful book *Last Child in the Woods: Saving Our Children from Nature-Deficit Disorder*, Richard Louv wrote, "Nature-deficit disorder describes the human costs of alienation from nature, among them: diminished use of the senses, attention difficulties, and higher rates of physical and emotional illness. This disorder can be detected in individuals, families, and communities. As we grow more separate from nature, we continue to separate from one another physically. An environment-based education movement—at all levels of education—will help students realize that school isn't supposed to be a polite form of incarceration, but a portal to the wider world."

As someone whose past life included thirty years of working within the so-called "criminal justice system," I am a strong believer in the healing, teaching, redemptive qualities of a nature-focused education. We can do a lot of good if we find ways to spend less time, money, and energy locking kids up and more time, money, and energy taking them outdoors and connecting them to nature and the best of their own human nature.

Sometimes the universe does scream at you. Uncertainty is within every heartbeat, so all we can do is be grateful for every thump. There is no such thing as a bad day on the river. There is no such thing as a bad day of being alive. Every day is a gift. Tailwaters, along mountain streams and lifetimes, have something in common, even though they may seem as if they are very different things. Both remind us that often what seems like the end of something is simply a temporary barrier to overcome. And both can teach us that resurrection is always possible; all we must do is flow. There is new life to be found on the other side of the wall.

Chapter Twenty

Devils

In poetry our motives are utterly similar to those who made cave paintings or petroglyphs, so that studying your own work of the past is to ruminate over artifacts, each one a signal, a remnant of a knot of perceptions that brings back to life who and what you were at that time, the past texture of what has to be termed as your "soul life."

~ *JIM HARRISON*

I GUESS WHEN YOU FEEL LIKE YOU'VE HAD THE SOUL KICKED OUT OF YOU, it seems natural that you might spend some time wandering around, looking up and down, and trying to find exactly where you lost it and how to put it back. We are souls with bodies, not the other way around. Without the essence of who we are—intact and authentically within our vessels—we are unblinking, inanimate objects; we are no longer soil. . . we are dirt.

Words are my petroglyphs. I scratch them out on a more or less durable rock. I paint them in colors wrung from nature like squeezing out my dreams and fingertip painting on my limestone self. They reflect and sustain my most noble nature. They are my tapping on the prison wall.

Whenever we gaze upon the artifacts of past lives, we gain perspective. It's so easy to slip into the illusion that life orbits around our own personal gravitational pull. It's easy to begin thinking that the universe owes us a living. It doesn't—*we* owe us a living. It's not a dress rehearsal. During this year, I have found broken pieces of my soul. I have steadfastly worked at not searching for the shards, and when I find them, I keep them in my pocket, not gluing anything together. I'm living thoughtlessly so that I might once again recognize myself . . . the original me, like a wren sees a hollow gourd. I've learned a lot in this year. I've learned that the way to get your soul back isn't to chase it but rather to quietly wait for it. When you're ready, it finds you.

It hasn't all been tranquil. Sometimes anything can wash up on shore: anger, sadness, fear, and that hollow, empty feeling that I used to have as a boy while hiding in the closet so I wouldn't be beaten. That closet was my shelter. It was my own true cave that protected me from the storm. In flashes, I remember that there was a spider in that closet and that just enough light slipped under the door so that I could see him dancing in the air. I was never afraid of him. I was afraid of the wounds we receive from those we trust and love and who are supposed to love us back. I was afraid of the betrayal. I was never afraid of him. He kept me company.

The worst part of suffering is being alone. Long after I left the Marines and years after all the dead faces came back to haunt me, I found out how alone someone can be, even when surrounded by those they love. They can't really help you. They may reach for you, but they don't know where you are, not really. It's not their fault. It's no one's fault. It's not even your fault. Still, it is our job to get up, dust off, and move on.

There was a time when I was afraid to go to sleep. I'd stay awake for as long as I could so the nightmares wouldn't come, but they always did. I'd wake up screaming and gasping for air in the dark with hot tears running down my face. It was no way for a Marine to act—I thought. I found myself wondering if I could go on, wondering if it wouldn't be easier to just let my truck drift into the cool autumn Hill Country air. I never thought I could think such things. It taught me compassion deeper than I had ever known. It taught me to recognize those same thoughts and feelings in the eyes of my wounded brethren at the Center for the Intrepid. It taught me how to tell them in a soft voice that they would be fine. I was given the power to tell them that life is beautiful, if you live it. By then, I had learned that when you are lost, you must go home.

The Texas Hill Country saved me. I stood in the river, and the water washed me clean. It flowed around my legs and up into me and filled up all the hollow, empty spots. And, the rivers made my hands stop shaking and my heart start beating and more than once they ran through that battered pump and dripped down my cheeks and then back into the river . . . back home. These rivers, canyons, and hills saved my life. I can't let them die. We can't let them die. There will be others who will need this place. These magical hills, canyons, and streams deserve to be told that everything will be fine and that they will remain alive and beautiful.

Rumi once wrote, "Let yourself be silently drawn by the strange pull of what you really love. It will not lead you astray." I have always been drawn to wild places. Even as a child, in wilderness, I have found peace. Within a breeze, I have felt something a transcendentalist might call "the breath of God." Wilderness has never let me down. It holds my hand. It looks into my eyes. It tells me, in a soft voice, that I will be fine. And this is why, at the turn of the year and the wee hours of my time remaining with Megan before she leaves for Scotland, I decided to drift to the Devil's River. We went together.

Historical records indicate that before the arrival of Spanish explorers in the late 1600s, the Indians of the region called the river "Dacate." The Spaniards named the river "San Pedro" after the Christian Saint Peter, in keeping with their tradition of the time. The origin and meaning of the Indian name are lost, and to this day, every river across the Texas Hill Country except the Devils has retained its Spanish name.

Legend has it that the Devil's received its name from former Texas Ranger Captain Jack Hays, who was leading an expedition to find the best route from San Antonio to El Paso. After leading his party across the dry hills and into the desert canyons he came to the river that his Mexican guide told him was named after Saint Peter. According to this account, Captain Hays responded, "Saint Pete, hell. This is the Devil's River."

I don't know if this story is true, but it is in keeping with the cultural history and worldview of the time. My ancestry reads like a map of Texas. I have Spanish, Anglo, Norman Irish, and Native American blood coursing through my veins. In truth, I feel a kinship with my Native American spirit rather than that of my Spanish, Anglo, Italian, and Norman predecessors. When I look upon these rivers, canyons, and hills, I do not feel the urge to exploit or conquer them; I feel the deep desire to connect with them.

The Texas Parks and Wildlife (TPWD) website describes the Devils River State Natural Area as "primitive and isolated" with "karst topography" that emits pure water from "numerous clear springs tumbling over limestone past rugged ridges, canyons and grassy banks, giving life to diverse plants and wildlife." Parks and Wildlife describes this region as "ecologically intact, free of impoundments, generally inaccessible, essentially primitive and unpolluted."

The Devil's River cuts through three biotic regions: the Chihuahuan Desert, the Edwards Plateau/Hill Country, and the Tamaulipan Desert. Finally, TPWD points out that the Devils River State Natural Area protects several "unique cultural and archaeological resources, including significant Lower Pecos style rock art." I think all these descriptions are well said, but there is so much more painted upon this landscape. This land is enchanted. This land is where the Texas hills meet the Mexican desert. It is not "empty." It is full of life and legend and lore. Let me take you there.

Our camp was far back in the hills with an arroyo behind it and cactus-studded rocky hills all around. After putting up my orange-colored tent, we promptly named it "Camp Pumpkin," and pleased with our surroundings, we jumped into the truck for the rough ride to the trailhead. The Devil's River lies at the end of almost thirty miles of rough dirt road from the nearest highway. (I hope the Park Service never paves that road.) The trailhead is nine-tenths of a mile from the river, so we had a beautiful hike through the desert hills before reaching our destination. (I hope the Park Service never allows vehicles to drive up to this river.) The Devil's River deserves respect. This river begs to be seen by foot or kayak; anything less is a perception-altering intrusion.

When we reached the top of the last hill, we could see the river below. It flowed clear and cold beneath the sycamores, live oaks, desert willows, and endless cobalt sky. The sounds of birds of every type and color were amazing. Two great kiskadees were screaming like monkeys in the treetops as vermillion flycatchers, painted buntings, hooded orioles, and black-chinned hummingbirds darted among the cactus. Red-eared slider turtles slipped into the river as we approached, and the funnel nose of a softshell turtle poked up for a breath of air. Racerunner lizards slithered along the pathway while spiny lizards hung upside down inside small cliffside caves. Looking straight up toward the sky, we saw black vultures riding the warm air currents just above the thousand-foot-high cliff face. The Devil's River is an oasis in the desert. It is magical.

Walking along the river's edge, we found a few nice spots to begin fishing. We chose a place where a long, shallow limestone shelf reached out into the river to the edge of a deep pool. We could hear tumbling water just upstream. I assumed it was a series of rapids or a waterfall, but I would soon find out that I was wrong. We sat on a rock and soaked our feet in the river while enjoying a pre-cast picnic. I always watch a river before I enter it. Like any new relationship, it's best to take it slow at first.

Stripping out some line, I made my first cast. In truth, I was barely paying any attention to the act of fishing. The sun illuminated the western hills, and the birdsong mixed with the treetop breezes so that we felt as if we were captured inside a dream. Almost immediately, I received a vicious strike, and my rod doubled over and throbbed with each head-shake and run. Then, leaping into the air, a bar-sided bronze-back finally came to hand. It was the first smallmouth bass I've ever caught.

The Devil's River has a genetically unique strain of native large-mouth bass, but it is known for the hard-fighting "smallies" that have been established here by Texas Parks and Wildlife. Megan gave me the thumbs-up sign and smiled ear to ear. We cast again.

There were several eruptions of smallmouth bass feeding en masse near Megan's casting spot. She was getting hits, but her timing was off, and she was missing the hookups. I, on the other hand, couldn't stop catching fish. Several bass and two amazingly beautiful yellow-bellied sunfish later and we decided to spend the remainder of the evening exploring the sound of running water just upstream. We reeled in and began walking along a limestone path near the river's edge. We never dreamed we would find a paradise just around the next bend.

A few hundred yards upstream, we came to the springs. When we first arrived and checked into the park, I instantly hit it off with Park Police Officer Roy. Like me, he had started out as a municipal police officer and decided life was too short to spend fighting drunks and punks. Now, he lives in the middle of thousands of acres of wilderness, where his home birdfeeder is covered in painted buntings and surrounded by wild turkey. He told us that if we walked a half mile upstream, we would come to the springs. He said we could fill our water bottles directly out of the mouth of each spring and that the water was completely pure. I never imagined how pristine this place would be.

The evening sunlight set everything off as if someone had lit a fire in the air. The desert vegetation was transformed into soft, green ferns that waved in the clear, gushing water that was pouring out of the cliff face every few yards. The water was markedly colder than that of the river. Deep winding cuts in the limestone substrate wound across the tide pool-like landscape between the desert cliff and the Devil's River.

We walked gently through the springs being careful not to step upon the myriad of waving aquatic vegetation or the hundreds of tiny fresh-water shellfish. Minnows darted and frogs jumped along the fresh cold-spring runs. Birds sang in the treetops with such fervor as to render us speechless. White-tailed deer watched us from the far riverbank. The sun edged toward China and away from Texas. We forgot about fishing. We forgot about time. We forgot about any fears or burdens we had originally brought with us. We remembered what joy felt like.

⸺•⸺

When we reached Camp Pumpkin, the sun had nearly set over the distant desert hills. Roy told us that we should watch for aoudad, mouflon, and Corsican sheep in the hills, and we did until the light grew too dim to see any detail at any distance. The wind had picked up a little and made lighting my Pocket Rocket camp stove a little iffy, but after a little adjustment, we had water boiling and made a nice dinner of Cuban rice, black beans, and coconut, which we ate under the starlight. At this point in the night, the moon shone large in the sky, and even with our headlamps turned off, we could see around the cactus and brush surrounding Camp Pumpkin. I kept a wary eye out for rattlesnakes seeking a warm bunkmate.

Lying on top of my sleeping bag at night, I watched the sky and tried not to sleep. Megan fell asleep quickly, and this pleased me as I knew we had had a wonderful long day with another one set to begin at sunrise. I am used to not sleeping. Insomnia sits on my shoulder each night and whispers in my ear. I have heard its voice every night since my time in the Corps. Still, on this night, I simply didn't want to miss the magic. At first, although the stars came out, they were somewhat subdued by the big three-quarter moon. I watched for hours, dozing off and waking, all the while noticing the moon's march across the seams of the tent screen and toward the purple-black horizon.

In time, the moon hid its amber face and left me wrapped within a primal cocoon of the universe. I spent that night watching the lights of the Milky Way as if it were for the last time. While I lay there looking up and in, I heard the rhythmic calls of crickets and frogs. I enjoyed their company. Still, in truth, I was hoping to hear the songs of coyotes coming from the starlit hills surrounding me. I was listening for the call of the wild as I have heard it before in the songs of wolves in Italy and their smaller cousins in many parts of the American West. And, even though they remained silent on that single night, I still felt their call, calling me home . . . in fact, I hear it now.

I am a captive to freedom. It holds me within its open arms. I find the songs of civilization as I do the scraping of a hickory box in springtime; there might be a promise of passion within the notes, but there is no love waiting upon arrival. The wild places I have known always capture me. They are a lover once held in younger years. It matters not how distant the reality; the memory remains real. I cannot wait until I see her once more. I am addicted to her. I am drawn to the sound of her rivers and the feel of her breezes. I am a wild man. Timidity offends me. My heart beats to the rhythm of wilderness.

With the slightest glow of morning, I put on my boots and stepped outside. It had grown cold in the wee hours, so I covered Megan and zipped up her sleeping bag. At one point during those same cold, ink-black, predawn moments, I stepped outside just to stand there surrounded by the Milky Way, looking up with outstretched arms, just taking it all in. I realized that I was, at that moment, the same image as the shaman cave paintings that adorn so many prehistoric shelters of this region. Did they feel the same power and wonder so many thousands of years ago? Did they, like me, stay awake so that they could worship these distant lights?

At sunrise, Megan woke, and we shared a simple breakfast of apple cinnamon Danish. We spoke in soft tones as if in a church because, really, we were. Gold-rimmed hills revealed ocotillo arms and cacti pads but no wild sheep. Montezuma and scaled quail darted between scrubby live oaks. Megan said that they looked like tiny feathered businessmen who were late for some important appointment. We broke camp and very reluctantly said "adios," wishing it good fortune until we return once more.

The hike from the trailhead to the river was pleasant and cool. We had seen the river at last light the day prior, and now we would fish it as it woke. The river was front lit in golden-bronze just yesterday, and now it rested in the shadow of the canyon wall. To the west, the semidesert hills shone brightly, and the sunlight painted the cliff-face edge in the same sunflower-yellow as a sunfish's belly.

We watched the river for a while before wading in and taking our first cast. It didn't take long before both Megan and I connected with nice smallmouth bass. We got a few aerial displays, but for the most part, the smallies seemed hell-bent on burrowing down into the water while trying to shake the fly free. Some of them succeeded in achieving a "long-distance release." It didn't matter, we were there for the fishing, not the catching. In fact, if we had not caught a single fish, the morning would have been just as special, the fish simply made it more so.

We worked our way up toward the springs, and for a short while, we both fished the area where the cold spring water tumbles into the Devil's River. I caught a few smaller colorful sunfish, and then as if on cue, we turned to each other and said, "This was perfect . . . let's stop and let perfect stay perfect."

We reeled in and snipped off our olive woolly buggers. I realized that, at that moment, although I had brought an assortment of streamers and poppers for this trip, we had done two days of fishing and caught many fish on the same two flies. On the evening prior, we had decided to meet Roy just before noon so that he could show us some of the ancient petroglyphs. I took one last look at the river. It was a bittersweet moment saying farewell. I had found a new friend . . . a new favorite place.

—

Megan and I climbed down the semi-sheer rock face, around sotal, oco-tillo, cat's-claw, and prickly pear. We balanced along the edges of life just as the ancient ones had done so long ago in this very same place. In the far distance, we could see the mountains of Mexico, home to black bear, Coues deer, and drug lords. In the near distance, we could see the arroyo where the ancient ones once gathered water. Burnt-orange rocks lay as scattered records of long-ago nights when sotol hearts were baked as images were painted in flickering light.

When we reached the cave, at first, all I noticed were the half-rubbed off linear images of deer. The aoudad sheep have discovered this cave, too, and are slowly rubbing away four thousand years of art with their bristle-haired backs. And then I looked up to the ceiling of the shelter and saw the red-painted shamans looking down upon me. It was as if they were waiting for me to personally find them.

I sat beneath the petroglyphs and looked out across the desert valley. I could feel the spirits of the ancient artists as if they sat beside me in the here and now. And, I believe they do. In an instant, they taught me of impermanence and of the importance of scratching messages and meanings upon any lifetime's walls. Art is the best of us; it is our DNA. It is how our better spirits touch generations. It is how "once upon a time" becomes timeless.

The Devil's River and the Canyonlands surrounding it reflect our national soul. The United States was the historical birthplace of the

National Park and Wilderness System concept. At the turn of the nineteenth century, we were the leaders in preserving what remains of wilderness. National parks from Africa to Asia were the result of our American leadership by example. Texas has done a good job of protecting many of its most valuable natural and archaeological treasures; but we must do more. This land is like a beautiful young woman sitting in a café, untouched and unchanged by the careless brutes that surround her. Once this condition changes, it cannot be undone. She will never smile again with the pure honesty of a desert flower.

Chapter Twenty-One

Just One More Cast

A work of art gives testimony to what it is to be a human being. It bears witness, it extracts meaning. A work of art is also the clearest nonphysical way that emotion is communicated from one human being to another. The emotion isn't referred to; it is re-created. The emotion shows us that our most private feelings are in fact shared feelings. And this offers us some relief from our existential isolation.
~ Stephen Dobyns

If the Earth and the heavens are canvases for the painting of any Great Spirit, if the hills and the rivers are the brush strokes of divinity, then our lives are such a canvas and, unless we make it otherwise, a work of art. Dripping paint may be our hallmark, and this is a fine thing as long as we meant to drip it and do so with power and purpose. But if we are merely careless with the number of beats our hearts make or breaths we take, then we are not artists, we are sinners. I know that it is a sin to let others define me. I choose the place where I stand and where my line drifts. It is a sin to let darkness diminish me; even in the moonlight,

I must keep casting. And I am sure that it is a sin that the river flows day and night, and I am not there to see it. So, I stand in the river beneath the endless sky and take one more cast.

This morning, a yellow mayfly landed upon the window of my truck. Like me, he was too far from the river. I told him, "Hold on, my friend, I'll take you home." I started the engine and began driving into the Texas hills. "Sometimes, the slightest things change the directions of our lives, the merest breath of a circumstance, a random moment that connects like a meteorite striking the earth. Lives have swiveled and changed direction on the strength of a chance remark." These words by Bryce Courtenay return to me. They are true, I think, except that some crossings are not chance, some endings are not random, and, if we pay attention, we can hear the universe as it tells us to wake up.

I decided that this memoir of person and place must end somewhere even if it never truly ends. I decided that the best place to complete the circle was the same place that this journey began. After all, this is nothing more than the story of the short, happy life of a single drop of water. Over and over, I hear the voice of the character Roy Batty in the movie *Blade Runner*. In his final moments, he sits in the rain, dying. His last words are, "All those . . . moments . . . will be lost in time, like tears . . . in . . . rain."

Today I went home to Lost Maples Canyon. I stood in the Sabinal River and cast across the wind. I caught and released many beautiful fish. I listened to the sounds of golden-cheeked warblers, black-capped vireos, scrub jays, and canyon wrens. I remembered my lost Marine brother Dave when we came here together, the last time I saw him alive. I remembered the silver-pink flashes of the rainbow trout connected to my line, the winter before last, and of how they had all perished in the heat of last summer. I remembered my first cast after my life changed forever. And I knew that this cast today was, in fact, the final cast of my most recent adventure . . . the end of this transformational year and the beginning of the new journey.

I arrived at the trailhead just as I had on the first day slightly over a year ago. Hiking up the East Trail toward the ponds, I came across three women with big binoculars watching the red-tailed hawk that nests each year on the cliffside. One was friendlier than the other two, but I don't blame them for that; they had no idea who I was. I told them of the best places to see golden-cheeked warblers, black-capped vireos, and painted and indigo buntings. I told them of where the Audubon's oriole lives, and that some wild turkey had been strutting along the road. Then, I said goodbye.

At the ponds, the wind blew hard through the canyon and over my shoulder. There are massive native largemouth bass in the ponds, but I never catch them. Between the tree limbs, the cliff face, and the cattails, it is just too difficult to reach the big ones with a roll cast. Still, I managed to send my little four weight line into the wind and into the dark, deep center of the pond.

I wasn't expecting much, and in truth, I wasn't paying much attention. Perhaps that is why I froze in place when a big bass charged out of the darkness, swallowed my fly, and then spit it out. Laughing out loud to myself, I cast back into the wind only to have a sycamore tree reach out and eat the fly. It was as if the canyon was telling me, "That's it . . . that was your chance." It didn't matter, I came for the fishing, not the catching.

I reeled in, and for a moment, I took the time to enjoy the sounds of the canyon. I listened to the sound of the Sabinal as it trickled over the limestone, in places only three feet across . . . small and beautiful, like any newborn. I listened to the sounds of the wind bending the trees and flapping the leaves and carrying the songs of canyon wrens. And then, I began walking back down the trail through the "Pooh Bear" woods toward the spot where the little stream tumbled over the cliff and along the limestone under the trees.

Stripping out some line, I tied on a number 10 foam grasshopper and began walking with as much stealth as I could manage up the canyon, casting to likely plunge pools as I went. Even though it is the beginnings of the Sabinal River, a river that reaches hundreds of miles downward until it touches the Gulf of Mexico, here it is a tiny, shallow stream. I had a few top water strikes from small yellow-bellied sunfish, but I missed everyone. It's okay, I don't fish here for the fish. I fish here for the solitude.

There is a pool just below the crossing that holds two nice Guadalupe bass and a few sunfish. In the hot, dry seasons, I just don't have the heart to cast to them, but we've had a bit of rain lately, and the water was high and cool. I decided to duckwalk my way up to the pool and send as soft a presentation as I could manage in their direction. My backcast looked pretty, as it stretched out along the canyon wall bending my golden glass rod. My forward cast felt on target, sharp, not too much power, with the hopper landing softly at the head of the pool. And, when it landed ever so softly, it made gentle ripples on the clear surface, which immediately sent both Guadalupe bass to the far edges of the pool like bullets to a tin can.

Picking up my cast, I sent the line forward once again, this time to the second pool. The hopper hit with a plop and immediately received a vicious strike from a flash of green and orange. My little rod doubled over, and in a moment, I brought a beautiful green sunfish to hand. Although I have fished every river and stream in the Texas hills, this is the only place I have ever caught green sunfish. I thanked him and sent him home, no worse for the experience.

On the walk back toward the main road, I contemplated a deep pool that is created where spring water spills out of the ground after a long stretch of subterranean travel. I decided to pass on it and continued to the pool where a Park Service bridge crosses the river. I could see a few good-sized Guadalupes in the pool along with an assortment of sunfish. Keeping a low profile, I cast the same little foam hopper onto the water with the same result, the bass swam quickly away, and a big green sunfish seized the fly. I brought him in quickly and slipped out the hook. He was so stunningly beautiful that I had to admire him for a moment before sending him home.

The "greens" have large bass-like mouths and angry, accusatory eyes. They were in the spawn, complete with fiery-edged fins and blue-green scales. Catching even one of these little fish is worth the price of admission.

Crossing the road, I saw a red-eared slider turtle doing the same. There was a lonely stretch of river cutting through the canyon that I wanted to try. Even from the road, I could see a few big bass cruising along the deeper pools. The water looked shallow near the crossing, so I stepped in and felt the instantly cool sensation of being submerged up to my waist. As is often the case in these Hill Country streams, the clarity of the water is deceptive.

It was so deep, in fact, that no matter how I tried, I could not reach the place where the bass were. The vegetation along the shoreline was too thick and too snaky looking to penetrate. I turned back, feeling a bit refreshed by my spring water-soaked shorts. I guess that is why the bass are so big.

I stopped for lunch under an old oak tree near the river. I drank spring water and ate a jalapeño-Jack-and-turkey sandwich while listening to birdsong and leaves rustling in the wind. When I'm fishing, I'm thoughtless. Just sitting here, I see memories. I think about the journey and what it means. I think about how much I have found my passions again . . . learning, teaching, and living.

During this year, I have eked out a meager living working multiple part-time teaching jobs at several universities. Thus far, I am still a part of the "new economy" . . . multiple contract jobs with no benefits. A week ago, I found out that several of my classes were being given away to a tenured faculty member, cutting my income by two-thirds and leaving me wondering, *Have I been right to follow this uncertain path?* "Yes," I replied.

After lunch, I walked to the first river crossing just inside the gate to the State Natural Area. The wind was whipping over my shoulder, and the water was way too deep to wade. I adjusted, clipping off the hopper, and I tied on a size 8 olive woolly bugger. This was my last cast. Looking back, I watched as if in slow motion while my rod bent backward, my line stretched into the wind, and then I sent everything I had forward, just to see what might happen next. Stripping the line once, then twice, I saw a dark form racing toward the fly just beneath the rippled water. My line grew taut, I raised the rod-tip, and the largest bluegill I have ever seen came to my hand a few moments later.

I have fished here in this river for decades. I have never caught a bluegill here before today. Last week, my wife Alice, Megan, and I went hiking along the Maple Trail for Megan's birthday. In several decades, I have only seen one or two golden-cheeked warblers. On that single day, we saw nine. That's how life is when you live it without expectation. It's full of surprises. And, if I had to lose those surprises by gaining the illusion of certainty once more, I would refuse that offer. It's not worth it. I do not want a life of safe, certain boredom.

Packing up my rod and gear, I began driving toward my little hometown of Boerne. I drove past the herds of bison and the flocks of wild turkey all frolicking in the yellow and blue wildflowers. I drove past Love Creek where the Nature Conservancy is saving a small piece of my homeland. I listened to Smokin' Joe Kubek playing the armadillo blues as I rolled up and down and around the hills. This one more cast was a good cast. I caught what I came to catch. Life is a tight loop suspended in midair.

I will never see this day again except in memories that fade and blend. But this day was lived well. It was spent well as each day must be spent, as if it were the last coin in my pocket. Dust to dust and water to water, in the end, I want to return to the river, and it matters not if it is my ashes that flow between the pocket water riffles or my body falls "belly flop-like" into the river, drifting like a heavy leaf. If this is my end, I say cheer for me, my friends; I got my wish. I took one more cast, and I am home.

I guess what's been bothering me these past few days is that after a year of fly-fishing through uncertainty, nothing is really "settled," and if I think about it, it's a little unsettling. I guess I've learned that the big questions have small answers. You don't save the world, just small pieces of it. Everything is a delaying action. Sometimes stepping over something rather than on it is the best you can do.

Perhaps fly-fishing through uncertainty didn't teach me anything about where I'm going or what comes next. Perhaps what I have learned is not where to go, but rather how to be. Perhaps this is the greatest lesson anyone can ever learn.

I have learned to be grateful. I have learned that hearing birdsong as the sun rises or sets and seeing starlight as I drift into dreams has more value than any artifact of human hands. We all live a mayfly life. We must live authentically now while we still have wings.

I have learned that I must let go of any expectation of fairness, and rather than expect justice, I must continue to give it no matter the outcome. I have learned the freeing power of forgiveness, and this includes forgiving myself. I have confirmed that courage and compassion are connected and that giving is reflective. Most of all, I have learned to make it my practice to embrace uncertainty. The price of wisdom is vision. Once truth is known, it cannot be unknown.

Even if I had captured the small yellow mayfly in my hand and released him into the breeze above the river, he would last only long enough to leave something of himself behind and send something forward in time. Drifting with the river where he was born, the seeds of his progeny return. His life, like my life, is brief. It is not tragic. It can be artistic if we choose living over existing. We are the same, he and I. In a lifetime that flickers within the space in between now and forever, we each make our mark, for what it's worth.

So, I scratch out these symbols to share moments of tragedy and triumph, uncertainty and resilience, hardship and hope. Perhaps, in the future, these symbols will fade. Perhaps, in time, like the petroglyph shamans, their meaning will be lost. It matters not.

What matters is that someday, some wounded warrior, young woman, or post-middle-aged man will be asking the same question . . . "What next?" And, they may seek shelter in these words and know that they are not alone in the universe. And they may feel as I have felt, that peace comes within a canyon wren's song, and the falling of maple leaves, and the beating heart of a wild leaping fish. Each of these miracles is not only a reflection of the moment but rather a window into many such moments lived in past lives and lives yet to come. We are not alone. We are all simply walking home—together. Life is beautiful. Enjoy the ride. No matter what comes, keep casting forward.

Epilogue

What if our religion was each other? If forests were our church?
If holy water—the rivers, lakes and oceans? If prayer was our words?
What if the Temple was the Earth? If our practice was our life?
What if meditation was our relationships?
If the Teacher was life? If wisdom was self-knowledge?
If love was the center of our being.

~ Ganga White

When I began this journey, I felt silent inside. It was that kind of silence you hear when the snow falls gently upon the earth, with no movement of air or water, and no voice of songbirds or humans, and even the voice inside you grows mute. I felt silent, like that. Before we can hear, we must learn to be silent. And when you lose faith in everything you ever believed in, you have nothing left to say, and so, you just listen. That's a good thing. It's a gift.

When my daughter began this journey, I know she was wondering, "What next?" What a gift it became that we both traveled across uncertainty together, and yet, we both found our own path. What a gift it was to stand in the river next to someone I love and cast toward whatever the current might bring. We both learned so much. We both learned so very much.

When you open such a gift, beautiful things can happen. You discover who your dearest friends are, and who they are not. You discover that you haven't lost the things that mattered most, because those things are within you and, therefore, only you can give them away. You discover the deep, deep reservoirs within you of resilience, loving-kindness, gratitude, determination, inspiration, and joy. You uncover your heart's truest desires and passions, and you learn to live them each day and to accept nothing less.

When this journey concluded, Megan had found her way. After earning her postgraduate degree in outdoor education in Scotland, she has created a beautiful life for herself teaching children about nature and the best parts of their own human nature. And yes, I miss my fishing buddy, but once or twice each year, we manage to stand in a river together, and when we do, we live lifetimes in a single day.

When this journey concluded, I found my way too. Using my written and spoken words, I have gone about the business of trying to help more people come to love and respect nature and themselves. I became a certified Texas Master Naturalist with Texas Parks and Wildlife and volunteer to teach inner-city children about nature and how being connected with nature can give them strength and hope. I teach college, conduct training, and write stories that are all intended to help others to first become silent, and then become the best versions of themselves. Often, I'm sure I must fail. Still, sometimes, I'm sure I succeed.

When you ask me, "How are you now?" I reply with the words of author George Monbiot: "For the first time in years, I felt that I belonged to the world. I knew that wherever life took me, however bleak the places in which I found myself might seem, that feeling—the sense of possibility, the sense of belonging—would remain with me. I had found hope where hope had seemed absent." In other words, "I am well, thank you." No matter what drifts by me, I simply keep casting forward. I hope you will too.

And finally, when this journey concluded, the Texas Hill Country, its canyons and streams, its flora and fauna were under more threat than ever from the impacts of largely human-induced climate change, human-introduced invasive species, human population expansion, and the endless human demand for water. There is much work to be done to save this beautiful historical landscape before there is nothing left to save. I hope this book helps more people to care and to act.

Acknowledgments

Dead Poets Society screenwriter Tom Schulman wrote, "No matter what anybody tells you, words and ideas can change the world." I believe this to be true. And although I do not expect this story of two people fly-fishing through life's uncertainty to change the world, I hope these words can change your worldview for the better, even just a little. If they do, there are people who have made this story possible, and without them, this book would have never reached your hands. Please allow me a moment to share my gratitude for the people who have supported me through this process and more.

One of the amazing things we learn during times of hardship is who our true friends are and who they are not. This is an important and potentially life-changing lesson. I am grateful to my lifelong friends, Janice "Lil Red" Bowden Hardaway, Margarita Quihuis, Cynthia Covey Cox, Monty Lambert, Pam Uschuk, Alx Stryker McCabe, Steven Philbrick, Tiffanie Castillo, Julie Herbot, James Leach, Julie Castleman, Nichole Bendele, and Maggie Serva for their unending support, kindness, and friendship. People like these give me hope for the world.

Ted Williams is a conservation writer whom I have admired for many years. His impeccably researched and powerfully written articles always seem to place truth over comfort and consistently present a call to action for the preservation and conservation of our natural world. If I were to choose two words to characterize Ted's written work, they would be honesty and courage. It was Ted who encouraged me to complete this book and submit it to Lyons Press, and then he generously agreed to write the foreword. I am grateful and honored for Ted's friendship, guidance, and support during this journey.

Artist, illustrator, writer, and professional fishing guide Bob White was instrumental in the publication of this book, and his friendship, kindness, and guidance have been a blessing to me. Bob is a gifted artist who translates meaningful moments into timeless images. There simply are not words to adequately express my gratitude to this man, my friend, Bob White.

I also want to thank Bill Bowers, Chris Wood, Kirk Deeter, and Dan Frasier for their friendship and support. I am grateful to Gene Brissie of Lyons Press for taking the time to read my story and then for choosing to bring it from the original manuscript to the completed literary work you now hold. And, I sincerely appreciate the guidance and support of my production editor, Kristen Mellitt, and Sean Sabo, my copy editor at Lyons Press.

Most of all, I am grateful to my wonderful wife and best friend of thirty-four years, Alice, and to our amazing daughter, Megan. They have both been the greatest joys and gifts of my life. Without them, I would not have become the man I am, nor would I have found the words to tell this story. I am a fortunate man, indeed.

Selected Bibliography

Ackerman, Diane. *The Human Age: The World Shaped by Us*. New York: W.W. Norton & Company, 2014.

Ackerman, Jennifer. *The Genius of Birds*. New York: Penguin, 2017.

Behnke, Robert J. *About Trout: The Best of Robert Behnke from Trout Magazine*. Guilford, CT: Lyons Press, 2007.

Davis, Wade. *River Notes: A Natural and Human History of the Colorado*. Washington, DC: Island Press, 2013.

Dillard, Anne. *Pilgrim at Tinker Creek*. New York: Harper Collins, 1974.

Enquist, Marshall. *Wildflowers of the Texas Hill Country*. Austin, TX: Lone Star Botanical, 1987.

Finch, Robert. *The Primal Place*. Woodstock, VT: The Countryman Press, 1983.

Haggerty, Michelle, and Meuth, Mary Pearl, eds. *Texas Master Naturalist*. College Station, TX: Texas A&M University Press, 2015.

The Handbook of Texas Online. Texas State Historical Association (TSHA), tshaonline .org. 1998.

Harari, Yuval Noah. *Sapiens: A Brief History of Humankind*. New York: Harper, 2015.

Hutchison, Kevin. *Fly-Fishing the Texas Hill Country: A Guide to Fishing and Lodging on Texas Rivers*. Smithville, TX: FishHead Press, 2008.

Kolbert, Elizabeth. *The Sixth Extinction: An Unnatural History*. New York: Picador, 2014.

Leopold, Aldo. *A Sand County Almanac: And Sketches Here and There*. New York: Oxford University Press, 1949.

Loflin, Brian, and Shirley Loflin. *Grasses of the Texas Hill Country*. College Station, TX: Texas A&M University Press, 2006.

Louv, Richard. *The Last Child in the Woods: Saving Our Children from Nature-Deficit Disorder*. Chapel Hill, NC: Algonquin, 2008.

McKibben, Bill. *Wandering Home: A Long Walk Across America's Most Hopeful Landscape*. New York: St. Martin's Griffin, 2014.

Monbiot, George. *Feral: Rewilding the Land, the Sea, and Human Life*. Chicago, IL: The University of Chicago Press, 2014.

Nash, Roderick F. *Wilderness and the American Mind, Fifth Edition*. New Haven, CT: Yale University Press, 2014.

US Global Change Research Program. *The Climate Report: The National Climate Assessment—Impacts, Risks, and Adaptations in the United States*. Brooklyn, NY: Melville House, 2019.

Weisman, Alan. *The World Without Us*. New York: Picador, 2007.

Williams, Florence. T*he Nature Fix: Why Nature Makes Us Happier, Healthier, and More Creative*. New York: W.W. Norton & Company, 2017.

Williams, Ted. S*omething's Fishy: An Angler's Look at Our Distressed Gamefish and Their Waters—And How We Can Preserve Both*. New York: Skyhorse, 2007.

Wrede, Jan. *Trees, Shrubs, and Vines if the Texas Hill Country: A Field Guide, Second Edition*. College Station, TX: Texas A&M University Press, 2006.

Praise for *Casting Forward*

"*Casting Forward* belongs alongside *Holy Ghost Creek* and *A Fly Fisherman's Blue Ridge* as books that perfectly capture the essence of place and our part in it. You would not be mistaken to say that this book is about the Texas Hill Country. Steve is, after all, a master naturalist, and a master storyteller. But *Casting Forward* is about so much more than the outdoors and nature. It is a story of one man's journey through rivers and mountains to live a life well lived and loved." —**Chris Wood, President/CEO, Trout Unlimited**

"Every bit the unique sort of Hill Country artistry as a Jerry Jeff Walker show at Gruene Hall. These words are incredibly honest, gritty, and melodic . . . sometimes rowdy, always soulful. Steve Ramirez has an uncanny knack for conveying the 360-degree perspective of fly fishing like only an author who has seen so much—and felt so much—can. He's an angling balladeer." —**Kirk Deeter, Editor-in-Chief, Trout Unlimited/Trout Media**

"In many ways Ramirez is the reincarnation of my late friend John Voelker, author of *Anatomy of a Fisherman* and the lesser work, *Anatomy of a Murder*. Both men were fleeing lives that had wounded them, and both found salvation in wildness through angling. A century hence *Casting Forward: Fishing Tales from the Texas Hill Country* will be referenced in the best of North American outdoor literature." —**Ted Williams, conservation journalist, author, and guide**

"*Casting Forward* by Steve Ramirez is an elegant ode to one of the great, lesser known fly-fishing regions of the United States—the Texas Hill Country. With every line of every chapter, Emily and I marveled at Steve's gifted vision of this river realm that we love so much and all its native treasures. Take a journey through the eyes of this unique warrior, fly fisher, and inspired writer . . . it might just be good for your soul." —**Dave Whitlock, author, artist, teacher, fly fisher**

"Ramirez guides us on a poetic and philosophical hike through the soul-healing adventure of a Marine whose duty is fulfilled, finding peace in the deep connections fly-fishing and nature provide. A true wordsmith, Ramirez offers vivid descriptions of scenery and water-scapes that bring us along as his fishing partner on these explorations of man's connection to the natural world, both on an individual and societal level." —**Dan Frasier, freelance writer and author of** *The Orvis Beginner's Guide to Carp Flies*

"*Casting Forward* moves between harsh reality and infinite possibility as easily as water moves between stone and sky. It asks questions of us—especially those pulled back by the past and yet pushed forward by time. If you stare long enough into an abyss, will it begin to stare into you? Are those capable of great violence the ones who speak most truly of kindness? And—in a voice that is at once sad and sweet and full of wonder—where is my river taking me now?

Casting Forward is rich in hard-won truths. That love of country must carry the emphasis on both words. That our redemption lies in being who we are in the place we love—and doing some small good in the world. It's a gem of a book." —**Peter P. Ryan, outdoor writer and photographer**

"Steve guides you through the eyes of a Marine seeking redemption through an uncertain world using fly fishing as a soul-washing experience. Steve will ignite your passion and challenge you through the world of fly fishing. Read this book!" —**Jack Dennis, author, fly fishing and fly-tying professional**